T0323817

Ethics, Meaning, and Market Society

This book explores the underlying causes of the pervasive dominance of 'unethics' in contemporary affairs in economics, business, and society. It is argued that the state of unethics is related to the overexpansion of market and market values in all spheres of social life and human activities. A correlate of this development is the emergence of an extremely individualistic, materialistic and narcissistic mind-set that dictates the decisions and behavior of people and organizations.

The author argues that art can help to overcome the dominant market metaphysics of our age, as genuine art creates models of 'poetic dwelling,' which can generate non-linear, progressive change that opens up a larger playing field for ethics. Aesthetics and ethics go hand in hand. Ethical action is not just right for its own sake, but makes the world a richer, livable and more beautiful place.

Ethics, Meaning, and Market Society will be of interest to students at an advanced level, academics, researchers and professionals. It addresses the topics with regard to ethics in economics, business, and society in a contemporary context.

Laszlo Zsolnai is Professor and Director of the Business Ethics Center at the Corvinus University of Budapest, Hungary. He also serves as President of the European SPES Institute in Leuven, Belgium.

Routledge Focus on Business and Management

For a complete list of titles in this series, please visit www.routledge.com/business/series/FBM

The fields of business and management have grown exponentially as areas of research and education. This growth presents challenges for readers trying to keep up with the latest important insights. Routledge Focus on Business and Management presents small books on big topics and how they intersect with the world of business.

Individually, each title in the series provides coverage of a key academic topic, whilst collectively, the series forms a comprehensive collection across the business disciplines.

ISSN: 2475–6369

Writing a Business Plan
A Practical Guide
Ignatius Ekanem

Manager vs. Leader
Untying the Gordian Knot
Robert M. Murphy and Kathleen M. Murphy

Accounting for Biological Assets
Rute Goncalves and Patricia Teixeira Lopes

Rising Consumer Materialism
A Threat to Sustainable Happiness
Afia Khalid and Faisal Qadeer

Evaluating IT Projects
Eriona Shtembari

Ethics, Meaning, and Market Society
Laszlo Zsolnai

Ethics, Meaning, and Market Society

Laszlo Zsolnai

Routledge
Taylor & Francis Group

NEW YORK AND LONDON

First published 2018
by Routledge
605 Third Avenue, New York, NY 10017

and by Routledge
2 Park Square, Milton Park, Abingdon, Oxon OX14 4RN

First issued in paperback 2021

Routledge is an imprint of the Taylor & Francis Group, an informa business

Publisher's Note
The publisher has gone to great lengths to ensure the quality of this reprint
but points out that some imperfections in the original copies may be
apparent.

Library of Congress Cataloging-in-Publication Data
A catalog record for this book has been requested

ISBN 13: 978-1-03-224196-8 (pbk)
ISBN 13: 978-1-138-63374-2 (hbk)

DOI: 10.4324/9781315207155

Typeset in Times New Roman
by Apex CoVantage, LLC

Contents

Tables

Preface

Hungarian writer Peter Müller once recalled something that his father, who had been a butcher in the 1930s in Budapest, had told him: "I was always honest in doing business; I never cheated my customers." Behaving unethically in business was simply unthinkable. Honesty was hardwired into his identity.

Today, being able to find this kind of uncompromising ethical behavior in business or other spheres of social life is almost unimaginable. This book discusses the new phenomena of globalization, privatization and financialization as the changing conditions of late modernity/contemporary capitalism and explores the underlying reasons for the pervasive dominance of 'unethics' in our contemporary affairs in business and society.

By *unethics* I refer to a state of affairs in which actors tend to eliminate or minimize any kind of ethical considerations from their decisions, activities or policies. I argue that unethics is related to market overreach and the dominance of market values in all areas of social life and human activity. A correlate of this development is the emergence of an extremely individualistic, materialistic and narcissistic mind-set that dictates the decisions and behaviors of people and organizations.

The result is an increase in social inequality, welfare malaise and moral transgressions on the one hand, and the drastic degradation of the biosphere (climate change, biodiversity loss and the collapse of ecosystems) on the other. The book discusses these topics in a holistic, multidisciplinary way.

I argue that *art* can help to overcome the dominant market metaphysics of our age. Genuine art creates models of 'poetic dwelling,' which can generate non-linear, progressive change and open up the playing field for ethics. English poet Percy Shelley once said that the great secret of moral conduct is "the identification of ourselves with the beautiful which exists in thought, action or person, not our own."

Aesthetics and ethics go hand in hand. Acting ethically is not just right for its own sake, but makes the world a richer, more livable and more beautiful place.

Part I

Why Unethics?

1   Introduction
Market Overreach

The central thesis of this book is that the overexpansion of the market and dominance of market logic in all spheres of social life is the main underlying cause of the 'ills' of our age.

As early as the 1940s Karl Polanyi warned that markets tend to dominate other spheres of social life, and induce the formation of a "market society" (Polanyi 1946). After World War II the overexpansion of the market received new impetus, and it has become pervasive in the last 40–45 years.

Globalization, privatization and financialization, the new conditions for late modernity/contemporary capitalism, inhibit economic actors from behaving in an environmentally sustainable and socially responsible way— that is, in a truly ethical way. The institutional system and its corresponding universe of values make ethical behavior virtually impossible, or contingent at best (Boda and Zsolnai 2016).

First, and at the core of the problem, is that *corporations* dominate the world of business (Korten 1995, Bakan 2005). Today, corporations are players in nearly every economic transaction. While the modern corporation has considerable merits, such as serving as a means to collect and unite into one organization the small investments of many individuals, it also has the inconvenient characteristic of dispersing and, ultimately, whitewashing responsibility. Limited liability also means limited moral liability.

> The situation may be contrasted with the case of unincorporated businesses, where unlimited liability also means unlimited moral liability. No distinction can be made by the business and the person(s) conducting it because the reputation of the one is the same as the reputation of the other.
>
> (Róna 2013: 10)

By nature, corporations and their owners have only limited responsibility.

The fact that corporations have many owners implies that individual shareholders do not necessarily have the power, or simply the interest, to control them, influence decisions, or hold management accountable. Shareholders are interested in dividends; that is, returns on investment. Dispersed ownership also creates a limitation on commitment towards the future of a company (one can sell one's shares at any time) and aggravates the dangers of a hostile takeover (Mayer 2013). Takeovers can easily happen, especially when corporations make long-term investments into the future that undermine their short-term profitability. Falling or stagnating share prices motivate owners to get rid of their shares. Therefore, the real aim of corporations cannot be anything but putting shareholder value above everything else. Lynn Stout (2012) calls this the "shareholder value myth." The shareholder value myth, together with the competitiveness myth, have devastating effects on the social and environmental performance of business (Tencati and Zsolnai 2010).

Today's extremely complex *financial system* blurs ownership and accountability and makes it impersonal. Institutional investors, investment funds and pension funds currently hold the large majority of corporate shares. Those institutions—generally corporations also—seek to increase profit at any cost. The financial crisis of 2008 revealed how derivatives and other complicated financial products mask reality, even from the eyes of experts. Nowadays, investors choose between investment portfolios offered by their banks or agents, and rarely know how their money works. One of the most effective ways to save on costs is to externalize them: to make nature, society and future generations pay.

Globalization creates a division between corporate decisions and stakeholders, owners and workers, consumers and places of production. This makes externalizing costs (i.e., causing social and environmental damage) easier. Globalization contributes to masking the real nature of business activity, and externalizing production costs (Princen 1997). The institutional setting of today's global capitalism helps to *dilute responsibility*, and leads to the aggravation of the 'tragedy of the commons' at a global scale.

The invasion of the market into almost all spheres of life inevitably destroys the intrinsic value of human activities, literally corrupting them. I show that there are two interrelated problems concerning the effect of the market on human activity: (i) the introduction of extrinsic forms of motivation (especially money) as an incentive for undertaking activity may crowd out the intrinsic motivation of actors, leading to a decrease in the quality of the output of activities; and (ii) measuring the success of activity in one dimension (money) tends to distort the goal of such activity and results in socially and ecologically degrading outcomes.

The 'genius of the market' should be acknowledged, but we must award it an appropriate role and restrict it to an appropriate size. This is possible if the financial component of non-market activities is reduced or eliminated, and success is measured in a more multidimensional, holistic way.

Karl Polanyi (1971) teaches us that it is not money-making but the provision of sustainable livelihoods that is the primary function of economic activities. This implies the rehabilitation of the 'substantive' view of the economy. According to this perspective, man survives by virtue of an institutionalized interaction between the human community and the natural environment. That process is the economy, which supplies man with the means of satisfying his or her needs.

Maximization of self-interest and free-market competition are the basic pillars of the Invisible Hand doctrine, belief in which is a prevailing theme of our age in the field of economics and beyond. The basic claim is that self-interested competitive forces bring benefit to all.

I use revealing cases to show that self-interest-based competition can result in environmental and social destruction. The first type of case is the 'tragedy of the commons,' which occurs when competing actors follow their narrow self-interest and thereby destroy the collective good on which their survival depends. The second type of case concerns the 'positional arms race,' which describes the situation when competing actors attempt to improve their own relative positions but arrive at a situation that is detrimental to them individually and collectively. The third type of case involves the 'tyranny of small decisions,' whereby a number of decisions, individually small in size and limited in time, cumulatively result in undesirable outcomes. The fourth type of case is the so-called phishing for phools. Here, economic players manipulate and deceive customers in the pursuit of profit, with no regard for the loss of customer welfare.

Moral disengagement mechanisms are today so prevalent in business and economic life (Bandura 2015). Corporations and other businesses engage in and create practices and products that violate legal and moral rules and take a toll on the public.

Economic actors tend to fool themselves in order to fool others. While the evolutionary benefits to deceiving others are obvious, it is problematic that it could ever be in the interest of an organism to deceive itself. However, the primary reason actors fool themselves is to fool others (Trivers 2011).

The encyclical letter of Pope Francis (2015), *Praise Be to You: On Care for Our Common Home* (*Laudato si'*), represents an excellent opportunity to build a new conversation about ecology and economics in an era called the Anthropocene in which humanity is altering the biogeochemistry of the Earth, destabilizing the climate and influencing co-evolution at the planetary level.

The most important suggestions in the encyclical include frugality of consumption and production, and acknowledging the intrinsic value of nature. Frugality implies rebalancing material and spiritual values in economic life (Bouckaert et al. 2008). This leads to the revival of the logic of sufficiency.

Also, we should think about nature as the 'commonwealth of life,' appreciating the uniqueness and interconnectedness of all life forms on Earth (Brown 2015).

Without respecting and nurturing 'place' we cannot achieve a state of ecological sustainability. Place-based organizations are not run on a purely materialistic basis. The non-materialistic features of a place (aesthetics, cultural heritage, community feelings, transcendence and so on) should be integrated into sustainability management. Place-based organizations break with the economic logic of efficiency and profit maximization, and organize their activities around the ideal of encompassing feelings of identity with and attachment to a place.

Important business, political and social decisions have an impact on the fate and well-being of people not yet born. Consequently, future generations have a stake in the present functioning of society. The imperative of responsibility (Jonas 1984) suggests that the present generation has a non-reciprocal duty to care for the future human beings who will be affected by its activities and policies.

Stakeholder theory says that organizations should consider the interests and claims of stakeholders and manage their activities accordingly. Using this perspective, the effective management of stakeholders is a strategic activity that is necessary for organizational success.

This book addresses two main problems related to stakeholder theory: (i) the narrow conception of stakeholders, and (ii) the fallibility of stakeholders concerning their own well-being. I argue that managing for a narrowly defined set of stakeholders is not a guarantee that the functioning of an organization will be sustainable in an ecological sense, or beneficial for wider society, including future generations. Considering the interest of stakeholders solely on the basis of their own considerations may lead to unacceptable outcomes. Organizations should thus expand the set of stakeholders they address, and look beyond stakeholders' self-reported interest.

Modern economics is a highly materialistic enterprise. Economic agents are considered to be individualistic beings who seek to maximize their material self-interest. Based on the principle of materialistic egoism, modern economies produced an enormous abundance of goods and services, but at huge ecological, social and psychological cost.

The economic teachings of world religions challenge the way economic actors function today. The conception of Jewish Economic Man, Catholic Social Teaching, Islamic economics, Hindu economics, Buddhist economics, and the theory of the Taoist economy represent life-serving modes of economizing which support the livelihoods of human communities and the sustainability of natural ecosystems. They inform and inspire spiritually grounded economic initiatives worldwide.

A post-materialistic business model (Zsolnai 2015) may help activate the intrinsic motivation of economic actors to serve the common good, and suggests that success should be measured in a more holistic, multidimensional way. In a post-materialistic economy, profit and growth are no longer the final ends, but only elements of a broader set of material and non-material goals. Similarly, cost-benefit calculations are not the only means of making corporate decisions but are integrated into a more comprehensive scheme of wisdom-based management.

This book claims that "Art Can Save the World". The core of market metaphysics is what Martin Heidegger calls 'calculative thinking.' According to Heidegger, poetic thinking represented by genuine art is the antidote to this kind of thinking. I argue that models of poetic dwelling can influence people and organizations to transform themselves into responsive and caring beings.

Beauty reveals itself as the illumination of the spirit in the material world. If utility considerations continue to precede aesthetics and ethics then utility itself will be destroyed. If we desire to live in a sustainable and well-functioning world, we must give priority to beauty and ethics over utility.

References

Bakan, J. 2005: *The Corporation: The Pathological Pursuit of Profit and Power*. New York: Free Press.

Bandura, A. 2015: *Moral Disengagement: How People Do Harm and Live with Themselves*. New York: Palgrave Macmillan.

Boda, Z. and Zsolnai, L. 2016: "The Failure of Business Ethics" *Society and Business Review* Vol. 11, No. 1, pp. 93–104.

Bouckaert, L., Opdebeeck, H. and Zsolnai, L. (Eds.) 2008: *Frugality: Rebalancing Material and Spiritual Values in Economic Life*. Oxford: Peter Lang Publishing.

Brown, P. G. 2015: "Ethics for Economics in the Anthropocene" in Brown, P. G. and Timmerman, P. (Eds.): *Ecological Economics for the Anthropocene: An Emerging Paradigm*. New York: Columbia University Press. pp. 66–88.

Jonas, H. 1984: *The Imperative of Responsibility: In Search of an Ethics for the Technological Age*. Chicago and London: The University of Chicago Press.

Korten, D. C. 1995: *When Corporations Rule the World*. San Francisco: Berrett-Koehler Publishers.

Mayer, C. 2013: *Firm Commitment: Why the Corporation Is Failing Us and How to Restore Trust in It*. Oxford, Oxford University Press.

Polanyi, K. 1946: *The Great Transformation: Origins of Our Time*. London: Victor Gollancz Ltd.

Polanyi, K. 1971: *The Livelihood of Man*. New York: Academic Press.

Pope Francis 2015: *Praised Be to You: On Care for Our Common Home*. Encyclical Letter *Laudato Si'* of the Holy Father Francis. The Vatican City.

Princen, T. 1997: "The Shading and Distancing of Commerce: When Internalization Is Not Enough" *Ecological Economics* Vol. 20, pp. 235–253.

Róna, P. 2013: "Ethics and the Limited Liability Corporation," Paper presented at the "Economic and Financial Crisis and the Human Person" workshop at the Von Hugel Institute, University of Cambridge, June 8, 2013.

Stout, L. 2012: *The Shareholder Value Myth: How Putting Shareholders First Harms Investors, Corporations, and the Public*. San Francisco: Berrett Koehler Publications.

Tencati, A. and Zsolnai, L. 2010: "The Collaborative Enterprise Framework" in Tencati, A. and Zsolnai, L. (Eds.) *The Collaborative Enterprise: Creating Values for a Sustainable World*. Oxford: Peter Lang Academic Publishers. pp. 3–14.

Trivers, R. 2011: *The Folly of Fools: The Logic of Deceit and Self-Deception in Human Life*. New York: Basic Books.

Zsolnai, L. 2015: *Post-Materialistic Business: Spiritual Value-Orientation in Renewing Management*. Basingstoke: Palgrave Macmillan.

Part II
The Mechanism of Unethics

2 The Market and the Corruption of Activities

In his influential book, *The Great Transformation*, Karl Polanyi (1946) describes the process by which the market takes over society and colonizes every segment of the life-world of people.

Philosopher Michael Sandel (2012) argues that the invasion of the market into almost all spheres of life inevitably destroys the intrinsic value of human activity, literally *corrupting* it.

There are two interrelated problems as concerns market effects on human activity: (i) the dominance of extrinsic forms of motivation (especially money) as a spur for doing activity may *crowd out* the intrinsic motivation of actors, leading to a decrease in the quality of the output of such activity; (ii) measuring the success of activity by using a one-dimensional term such as *monetary value* may distort the goal of activity and result in socially and ecologically degrading outcomes.

2.1 Money as Motivation

Having money as the main motivation for human activity is dangerous, as it can decrease the intrinsic motivation of actors, leading to a decrease in the quality of outputs. Additionally, a focus on money cultivates a self-centered value orientation, which results in socially insensitive and ethically irresponsible behavior.

The theory of 'crowding out' shows why using money as a form of motivation may be counterproductive. A monetary reward offered or expected tends to crowd out individual willingness to perform a task for its own sake (i.e., based on intrinsic motivation) if an actor's sense of recognition, fairness or self-determination is negatively affected. The *crowding-out effect* of pricing may also spill over into sectors where pricing is not typically applied (the 'spillover effect') if the persons affected find it costly to distinguish between sectors. The crowding-out of motivation and this spillover effect narrow the scope for successfully applying monetary rewards (Frey 1997).

The impact of the crowding-out phenomenon has important consequences for Adam Smith's famous statement that we can expect to obtain our bread not through the benevolence of the baker but from his self-interest. Certainly, expectations of making a profit strongly incentivize the baker, but producing truly healthy and beautiful bread requires something different: priority must be awarded to intrinsic commitment over monetary reward. The dangerous and unsustainable practice of modern agribusiness is an illustrative example of this (Zsolnai and Podmaniczky 2010).

Psychologist Gianvittorio Caprara, through developing a scale to assess civic moral disengagement, shows empirically that cultivating greed leads to the manipulation of others and oneself. The empirical findings of Caprara and his team suggest that if agents become self-interested, then it is likely that their self-exonerative maneuvers will do *harm* to *others*. To further the common good we need agents who care about and pursue both self-interest and community interest (Caprara and Campana 2006).

2.2 Money as a Measure of Success

The metric 'financial profit' is inadequate as the sole indicator of the success of human activity. Monetary calculations provide an incomplete and biased evaluation of activities. Such a metric reflects the values of the strongest stakeholders, favors preferences in the here and now, and presupposes the reducibility of all kind of values to monetary ones.

The market as a mechanism for evaluating decisions and actions is inherently deficient. First of all, there exist *stakeholders* who are simply *unrepresented* in the market determination of value. Natural beings and future generations have no opportunity to vote in the marketplace. Second, the preferences of human individuals count rather unequally; that is, in proportion to their purchasing power—the interests of the poor and disadvantaged are necessarily *underrepresented* in free-market settings. Third, the actual preferences of market players are rather *self-centered* and *myopic*; that is, economic agents make decisions regarding only short-term consequences.

Using monetary terms as the sole criterion for judging human activity implies *strong commensurability*, meaning that there should exist a common measure of different values based on a cardinal measurement scale. Mainstream economics suggests that values that are outside the traditional market should be calculated by using shadow prices and other market-based evaluation techniques. In this way, externalities can be 'internalized' and the full-cost pricing of activities can be developed.

However, ecological economists have demonstrated that the claim for the strong commensurability of values is invalid. The value of natural assets cannot adequately be expressed in monetary terms (McDaniel and Gowdy

2000). Similar arguments can be developed for important human and social values, such as health and safety, ethics and aesthetics.

To be able to judge the total value of any human activity, we need to incorporate a number of non-financial value-criteria, in addition to traditional measures. The following scheme is an illustration of such a multidimensional and holistic evaluation procedure.

The underlying idea of project evaluation is that a project is worthy of being undertaken if and only if the state of affairs *with* the project is better than the state of affairs *without* the project.

Let **P** be a project whose *total monetary cost* is p*. Let **Q** be the original state of affairs (that is, the state of affairs without the project). Let **Q*** be the new state of affairs (the state of affairs with the project).

There are two alternative uses of the money p*. One is to use it to finance project **P**. The other is not to undertake project **P** but use money p* to finance other projects, such as investing in treasury bonds.

Let **d(P)** be the discounted cash flow that project **P** can produce for a given period of time. Let **d(p*)** be the discounted total earnings of money p* for the same period of time. So **d(P)** and **d(p*)** represent two alternative uses of the same amount of money.

Let **E ( )** be a value function by which the state of affairs can be evaluated using an ordinal scale from the *ecological point of view*.

$$\text{(I) } \mathbf{E(Q)} = \begin{cases} 1 & \text{if the state of affairs } \mathbf{Q} \text{ is beneficial to nature;} \\ 0 & \text{if the state of affairs } \mathbf{Q} \text{ is neutral with regard to nature;} \\ -2 & \text{if the state of affairs } \mathbf{Q} \text{ is harmful to nature.} \end{cases}$$

Let **S ( )** be value functions through which the state of affairs can be evaluated using an ordinal scale from the *social point of view*.

$$\text{(II) } \mathbf{S(Q)} = \begin{cases} 1 & \text{if the state of affairs } \mathbf{Q} \text{ is good for society;} \\ 0 & \text{if the state of affairs } \mathbf{Q} \text{ is neutral with regard to society;} \\ -2 & \text{if the state of affairs Q is bad for society.} \end{cases}$$

Let **M ( )** be a *monetary value function*, as follows:

$$\text{(III) } \mathbf{M(P)} = \begin{cases} 1 & \text{if the discounted cash flow } \mathbf{d(P)} \text{ is positive;} \\ 0 & \text{if the discounted cash flow } \mathbf{d(P)} \text{ is zero;} \\ -2 & \text{if the discounted cash flow } \mathbf{d(P)} \text{ is negative.} \end{cases}$$

The following vector provides an overall evaluation of the original state of affairs.

(IV) $[E(Q), M(p^*), S(Q)]$

where **E(Q)** and **S(Q)** represent the environmental and the social evaluation of the original state of affairs, and **M(p*)** represents the monetary evaluation of not undertaking the project.

The overall evaluation of the new state of affairs is provided by the following vector.

(V) $[E(Q^*), M(P), S(Q^*)]$

where **E(Q*)** and **S(Q*)** represent the environmental and social evaluation of the new state of affairs, and **M(P)** represents the monetary evaluation of the project itself.

The sufficient condition for undertaking the project is the following:

(VI) $[E(Q^*), M(P), S(Q^*)] \Rightarrow [E(Q), M(p^*), S(Q^*)]$

This means that the state of affairs with the project is *better* than the state of affairs without the project when environmental, monetary, and social values are considered simultaneously. Social choice theory may help us to make decisions in situations like (VI) when different components of the vectors are not necessarily comparable. The crux of the matter is that we should extend the informational basis of analyses and broaden the evaluative space beyond monetary values to include ecological and social values that cannot adequately be translated into monetary terms.

Meeting this condition will protect against the overexpansion of markets and market logic into non-market spheres of social life. The "genius of the market" (Kay 2002) should be acknowledged. The point is to find the appropriate role and size for markets. This is possible if monetary considerations are reduced or eliminated from non-market activities, and success is measured in a multidimensional, holistic way.

2.3 The Substantive Meaning of 'Economic'

Karl Polanyi (1977) distinguished between the formal and the substantive meanings of the term 'economic,' arguing that the *formal* meaning springs from the logical character of a means-ends relationship. From this meaning springs the focus on scarcity in the traditional definitions of economics. In contrast, the *substantive* meaning of 'economic' highlights the elemental fact that human beings, like all other living things, cannot exist without the physical environment that sustains them. So, in the substantive sense, 'economic' denotes nothing other than bearing reference to the process of satisfying the material needs of a community.

Taking the substantive view of the economy has huge implications for modern society. It means that cost-benefit calculations should not be used to decide the rightness of human activities—only by using substantive criteria (namely, sustainability, and pro-socialness) can we guarantee that human activities are 'right.'

Polanyi (1946) also introduced the concept of "fictitious commodities" to describe entities such as land, labor and money whose production does not (and cannot) satisfy the laws of supply and demand. Land represents nature, labor represents people and money represents a measure of value. These primordial entities, so vital for the functioning of the economy, are created and destroyed by laws other than those of the market, and any attempt to consider and manage them as commodities will simply destroy them. To sustain nature, people and money we should go beyond the logic of the market.

Polanyi (1977) suggests that the true function of the economy is to support the *livelihood of man*. Man survives by virtue of the institutionalized interaction between human communities and the natural environment. That process of interaction is the economy, which supplies humanity with the means of satisfying its needs. Polanyi teaches us that it is not money-making but the provision of a sustainable livelihood that is the primary function of economic activity.

References

Caprara, G-V. and Campana, C. 2006: "Moral Disengagement in the Exercise of Civic-Ness" in Zsolnai, L., Boda, Z. and Fekete, L. (Eds.): *International Yearbook of Business Ethics*. Oxford: Peter Lang. pp. 83–94.

Frey, B. 1997: *Not Just for the Money: An Economic Theory of Personal Motivation*. Cheltenham: Edward Elgar.

Kay, J. 2002: *The Truth about Markets: Their Genius, Their Limits, Their Follies*. London: Penguin.

McDaniel, C. and Gowdy, J. 2000: *Paradise for Sale: Regaining Sustainability—a Parable of Nature*. Berkeley: University of California Press.

Polanyi, K. 1946: *The Great Transformation: Origins of Our Time*. London: Victor Gollancz Ltd.

Polanyi, K. 1977: *The Livelihood of Man*. New York: Academic Press.

Sandel, M. 2012: *What Money Can't Buy: The Moral Limits of the Markets*. London: Allen Lane.

Zsolnai, L. and Podmaniczky, L. 2010: "Community Supported Agriculture" in Tencati, A. and Zsolnai, L. (Eds.): *The Collaborative Enterprise: Creating Values for a Sustainable World*. Oxford: Peter Lang. pp. 137–150.

3   When the Invisible Hand Fails

Self-interest maximization and free-market competition are the basic pillars of the *Invisible Hand* doctrine, which is the prevailing belief of our age. The basic claim of the doctrine is that self-interested competitive forces bring benefit to all. But overwhelming evidence shows that the working of the Invisible Hand is the exception rather than the general rule.

I will illustrate how self-interest-based competition can result in destruction using four important types of cases. The first type of case is the well-known *tragedy of the commons*, which occurs when competing actors follow their narrow self-interest and thereby destroy the collective good on which their survival depends. The second example is the case of the *positional arms race*, which describes when competing actors attempt to improve their own relative positions but arrive at a situation that is detrimental to them individually and collectively. The third case involves the *tyranny of small decisions*, whereby a number of decisions, individually small in size and short-term, cumulatively result in an outcome that is neither optimal nor desirable. The final type of case is so-called *phishing for phools*, where economic players manipulate and deceive their customers to make a profit, with no regard for loss of customer welfare.

The commonly accepted understanding of the Invisible Hand doctrine reads as follows: if individual actors follow their own self-interest in a competitive setting, then this will produce the optimal outcome for them collectively (Samuelson and Nordhaus 1989). Conventional economic theory raises some important critiques of the doctrine and indicates why the beneficial effect of the market's Invisible Hand is limited. These factors include the existence of externalities, imperfect information and an undersupply of public goods (Stiglitz 2007).

3.1 Tragedy of the Commons

The well-known tragedy of the commons model (Hardin 1996/1968) shows how self-interested individuals in free competition destroy their own shared resources and ruin themselves. The model describes an open pasture on which each herdsman tries to raise as many cattle as possible, with the total number of grazing animals remaining within the carrying capacity of the pasture. The situation remains stable as long as wars, epidemics and other phenomena keep the number of grazing animals at a sustainable level. However, when these population-reducing factors are absent, the system becomes unstable and every rational herdsman is incentivized to put ever more cattle onto the pasture—by doing so, they will obtain a greater share of profit for themselves, while distributing the costs (i.e., the effects of overgrazing) among all the other herdsmen. Since the positive individual utility of adding one more animal is nearly +1, and the negative utility is only a fraction of -1, the rational herdsman in endeavoring to maximize his gain has no other rational choice than to keep increasing the number of cattle he keeps on the common land. The result is overgrazing, which brings ruin to all.

The tragedy of the commons does not always occur. Ostrom (1990) describes various cases of the sustainable management of local natural resources that illustrate the fact that the emergence of cooperative strategies among all actors involved is another potential outcome. The author provides concrete examples of how stable self-governing institutions have solved problems linked to common-pool resources, including high mountain meadows in Switzerland and Japan, irrigation systems managed by farmers in Spain and irrigation communities in the Philippines. With these local, community-based management models founded on cooperation, collective rights-of-use replace exclusive property rights and market relations, and ensure the sustainable exploitation of natural resources.

Ostrom's investigation concerns local-scale problems with common-pool resources. The current planetary-scale environmental problems—climate change, biodiversity loss, the plundering of natural resources—may be more adequately described using Hardin's model.

3.2 Positional Arms Race

Based on behavioral evidence, Robert Frank claims that the failure of the Invisible Hand is nearly inevitable, as there is an inherent conflict between the interests of the individual and the interest of the community as a whole (Frank 2011).

Darwin was one of the first scientists to recognize the conflict that is inherent between individuals and the species to which individuals belong. Frank notes that in such cases of conflict, individual interests triumph over the interest of the species. He uses the example of bull elephant seals to illustrate how the pursuit of short-term interest leads a group, as a whole, to achieve sub-optimal outcomes.

Bull elephant seals grow to a massive size, potentially weighing over 6,000 pounds and exceeding 20 feet in length. Female elephant seals, in contrast, weigh only 800–1,200 pounds, or one-fifth of the weight of males. This excessive disparity in size results from an evolutionary 'arms race' to obtain an advantage in mating—males fight viciously with each other over females. However, the gigantic size of males, which gives them an advantage in fights, is a disadvantage in other areas. Male seals are sluggish and vulnerable to attack by other predators such as sharks and humans. Nonetheless, any bull that weighed much less than the others would never find a mate (Frank 2011).

In terms of the human economy, Frank shows that people care more about relative wealth than absolute wealth. They engage in social comparisons with their peers that results in a positional arms race for income, property and other objects of social status, leading to states of accumulation that go beyond the optimal level of ownership of these positional goods (Frank 2011).

3.3 The Tyranny of Small Decisions

The tyranny of small decisions describes a phenomenon whereby a number of decisions, individually small in size and short-term, cumulatively result in outcomes that are neither optimal nor desirable. Kahn (1966) describes the problem as a common issue in market economics, and one that can lead to market failure.

Ecologist William Odum (1982) extended the notion of the tyranny of small decisions to environmental issues. He states that environmental problems can be traced to decisions that resulted from a series of small decisions.

In the case of the tyranny of small decisions the Invisible Hand fails when a series of small, individually rational decisions negatively change the context of subsequent choices, even to the point where potentially desirable alternatives are irreversibly destroyed.

3.4 Phishing for Phools

Nobel-prize-winning economists George Akerlof and Robert Shiller (2015) demonstrate that when opportunities arise in a free economy, 'phishers' are always there to manipulate and deceive customers. They engagingly document this phenomenon in the markets for alcohol, tobacco, gambling, food, houses, cars, pharmaceuticals and financial products.

Akerlof and Shiller identify two main origins for phishing: one is distorted information and the other psychological biases. In the case of information pools, customers act on information that is intentionally crafted to mislead them. In the case of psychological pools, the emotions of customers override the dictates of common sense, or cognitive biases lead them to misinterpret reality as the basis for their action. Economists believe that regulation may help to avoid information pools, but are somewhat puzzled about how to reduce psychological pools.

3.5 Alternative Solutions

Referring to evolutionary theory, D. S. Wilson and John M. Gowdy (2014) show that acting on self-interest does not robustly benefit the common good. The general rule is that the adaptation at any level of a multi-tier hierarchy requires a process of selection at that level, and tends to be undermined by selection at lower levels. Accordingly, evolutionary theory does not support the received version of the Invisible Hand, which suggests that society works best if individuals are allowed to act in their own economic interest.

To avoid the tragedy of the commons, the positional arms race, the tyranny of small decisions, and phishing for phools we need to pursue alternative solutions, including developing and maintaining governance structures that curb the excesses of the market and promote and reinforce the pro-social behavior of agents that protect the common good.

The behavior of economic actors can be enriched and moderated by adopting explicit *moral considerations* (Rona and Zsolnai (Eds.) 2017). Pro-social actors who consider the well-being of others and the wider environment will be less likely to engage in practices that destroy the common good.

References

Akerlof, G. and Shiller, R. J. 2015: *Phishing for Phools: The Economics of Manipulation and Deception*. Princeton and Oxford: Princeton University Press.

Frank, R. 2011: *The Darwin Economy: Liberty, Competition, and the Common Good*. Princeton and Oxford: Princeton University Press.

Hardin, G. 1996/1968: "The Tragedy of the Commons" in Castro, B. (Ed.): *Business and Society*. Oxford: Oxford University Press. (Originally published in 1968). pp. 1243–1248.

Kahn, A. E. 1966: "The Tyranny of Small Decisions: Market Failures, Imperfections, and the Limits of Economics" *Kyklos* Vol. 19, pp. 23–47.

Odum, W. E. 1982: "Environmental Degradation and the Tyranny of Small Decisions" *BioScience* Vol. 32, No. 9, pp. 728–729.

Ostrom, E. 1990: *Governing the Commons. The Evolution of Institutions for Collective Action*. Cambridge: Cambridge University Press.

Rona, P. and Zsolnai, L. (Eds.) 2017: *Economics as a Moral Science*. Springer.

Samuelson, P. A., and Nordhaus, W. D. 1989: *Economics*. New York: McGraw Hill.

Stiglitz, J. 2007: *Making Globalization Work*. New York: W.W. Norton & Company.

Wilson, D. S. and Gowdy, J. M. 2014: "Human Ultrasociality and the Invisible Hand: Foundational Developments in Evolutionary Science Alter a Foundational Concept in Economics" *Journal Bioeconomics* Vol. 17, pp. 37–52.

4   Moral Disengagement

In an experimental study, Armin Falk and Nora Szech (2013) demonstrate that using the *market* as a *frame of reference* provides a good excuse for people to morally disengage from considerations of doing harm and damage to third parties. Such insight underscores how the level and type of moral disengagement that occurs in business is uniquely problematic.

Moral transgressions are well-known in today's business world. Many corporations are involved in violating legal and moral rules through developing products and following organizational practices that take a toll on the public. The social cognitive theory of moral agency, developed by Bandura (1986), provides a conceptual framework for analyzing how otherwise pro-social managers adopt socially injurious corporate practices. This is done through a type of selective moral disengagement that is seen in many cases of corporate misconduct—examples range from the Bhopal industrial accident involving Union Carbide to the Ford Pinto case, the Nestlé infant formula controversy, the Three Mile Island nuclear power plant event, the Enron and WorldCom scandals of the 2000s and, more recently, the wrongdoing witnessed during the financial crisis.

World-renowned psychologist Albert Bandura's social cognitive theory offers a robust model of moral agency (Bandura 1986). In this model, moral thought and self-evaluative reactions, moral conduct, and environmental influences operate as interacting determinants of each other. Within this triadic model of reciprocal causation, moral agency is exercised through self-regulatory mechanisms. Transgressive conduct is regulated by two sets of sanctions, social and personal. Social sanctions are rooted in the fear of punishment by external actors; self-sanctioning operates in response to self-condemning reactions to one's own misconduct (Bandura 1990).

Bandura discovered a number of psycho-social mechanisms by which moral control can be selectively disengaged from detrimental conduct. These mechanisms of moral disengagement enable otherwise considerate people to commit transgressive acts without experiencing personal distress and guilt.

Using the words of evolutionary psychologist Robert Trivers (2011), people "fool themselves" in order to "fool others."

The eight moral disengagement mechanisms identified by Bandura (1990) are the following:

Moral justification. People do not ordinarily engage in reprehensible conduct until they have justified to themselves the rightness of their actions. During the process of moral justification, detrimental conduct is made personally and socially acceptable by portraying it as having valuable social or moral purpose.

Euphemistic labeling. Activities can be perceived in markedly different ways depending on what they are called. Euphemistic labeling can mask reprehensible activities, or even confer respectable status upon them. Through sanitized and convoluted language, destructive conduct is made benign, or at least acceptable.

Advantageous comparison. By contrasting one's own behavior with that of another, perceptions can be modified. Through exploiting advantageous comparisons, injurious conduct can be rendered benign, or made to appear to be of little consequence. The more extreme the activities one's own are contrasted with, the more likely it is that personally injurious conduct will appear trifling, or even benevolent.

Displacement of responsibility. Individuals may view their action as springing from (or condoned by) the social pressures or dictates of others such as a legitimate authority, rather than as something for which they are personally responsible, thereby sparing themselves self-censuring reactions. Through this process of displacing responsibility individuals may be willing to behave in ways they would normally repudiate.

Diffusion of responsibility. The exercise of moral control is weakened when personal agency is obscured by the diffusion of responsibility for detrimental conduct. Harm done by a group may be attributed in large part to the behavior of others. People may behave more cruelly when a group can be held responsible than when they may be held personally accountable for their action.

Disregarding or distorting consequences. When individuals pursue activities harmful to others for personal gain, or because of social inducement, they may avoid facing up to the harm they cause. In addition to paying selective inattention to and cognitively distorting any effects, such misrepresentation may involve an active effort to discredit evidence of any harm that has been caused.

Dehumanization. Self-censure for injurious conduct can be disengaged or blunted by a process of dehumanization that divests victims of human qualities, or attributes animal-like qualities to them. Once dehumanized, individuals may no longer be viewed as persons with feelings, hopes and concerns, but as subhuman objects.

Attribution of blame. Blaming one's adversaries or circumstances is another expedient that can serve self-exonerating purposes. By fixing the blame on others or on circumstances, not only are one's own injurious actions excusable, but also one can even feel self-righteous.

Bandura (2016) extensively documents how these mechanisms are at work in a wide range of areas of life in the USA and beyond: gun manufacturers, the entertainment industry, tobacco companies, finance and banking, terrorism, climate science and more. The large body of evidence presented by Bandura has important implications for the naive belief that the market will create sufficient incentive to encourage morally responsible conduct.

In a piece of research, Robert A. Baron et al. (2015) demonstrate that the motivation for entrepreneurs to make financial gains is positively related to moral disengagement, which itself is positively related to the tendency to make unethical decisions. Overwhelming market and financial forces and the corresponding goals of personal self-enhancement lead to morally disengaged behavior.

Business ethics is a countervailing force for stopping or at least reducing the use of moral disengagement strategies. However, the conventional tools of business ethics (such as ethical codes, ethics officers, ethics training programs and the like) appear to be ineffective at counteracting the strong moral disengagement of today's business, political and intellectual leaders. A more critical and enlightened approach to business ethics is clearly needed (Bandura et al. 2000).

One worthwhile task would be to monitor and publicize organizational practices and policies that have detrimental effects on humans. The more visible the consequences on the affected parties for decision-makers, the less likely it is that they can be disregarded, distorted or minimized for long. Another task is to increase the transparency of the discourse by which the deliberation of organizational policies and practices are created. The more public the discourse about decisions and policies, the less likely leaders are to justify reprehensible conduct by their organizations.

Diffused and ambiguous structures of responsibility make it easy to discount personal contributions to harmful effects. *Instituting* clear lines of *accountability* can help curtail moral disengagement. Exposing *sanitizing language* that masks reprehensible practices is still another corrective. Affected parties must be *personalized,* and their concerns *publicized* and addressed.

Bandura ends his latest book with dramatic words by claiming,

> To function humanely, societies must establish social systems that uphold compassion and curb cruelty. Regardless of whether social practices are carried out individually, organizationally, or institutionally, it should be made difficult for people to delete humanity from their actions.
>
> (Bandura 2016: 446)

I agree with this statement. The final recourse for ethics is to appeal for and capitalize on the individuals' own sense of humanity.

References

Bandura, A. 1986: *Social Foundations of Thought and Action: A Social Cognitive Theory*. Upper Saddle River, NJ: Prentice Hall.

Bandura, A. 1990: "Mechanisms of Moral Disengagement" in Reich, W. (Ed.): *Origins of Terrorism: Psychology, Ideologies, States of Mind*. Cambridge: Cambridge University Press; Prentice Hall, NJ: Englewood Cliffs. pp. 45–103.

Bandura, A. 2016: *Moral Disengagement: How People Do Harm and Live with Themselves*. New York: Macmillan.

Bandura, A., Caprara, G. V. and Zsolnai, L. 2000: "Corporate Transgressions through Moral Disengagement" *Journal of Human Values*, Vol. 6, No. 1, pp. 57–64.

Baron, R. A., Zhao, H. and Miao, Q. 2015: "Personal Motives, Moral Disengagement, and Unethical Decisions by Entrepreneurs: Cognitive Mechanisms on the 'Slippery Slope'" *Journal of Business Ethics* Vol. 128, pp. 107–118.

Falk, A. and Szech, N. 2013: "Morals and Markets" *Science* Vol. 340, pp. 707–711.

Trivers, R. 2011: *The Folly of Fools: The Logic of Deceit and Self-Deception in Human Life*. New York: Basic Books.

Part III

Nature and Future Generations

5 Integral Ecology and Sustainability

The overreach of market activities and moral disengagement of economic players has led to the currently devastating state of the Human-Earth system, characterized by climate change, biodiversity loss and ecosystem collapse on the one hand, and social inequality, mass poverty and social disorder on the other. David Orr (2016) states that the situation is so serious that the survival of humanity is at stake. This is not an exaggeration.

5.1 The New Reality of the Anthropocene

As consumption and the human population have increased, humankind has ushered in a new era: the so-called Anthropocene (Crutzen 2002, Steffen et al. 2011). This term describes a time in which humanity is altering the biogeochemistry of the entire planet, destabilizing the climate and influencing co-evolution at the planetary level. The conditions of the Anthropocene appear to represent a regrettable departure from the relatively placid past 10,000 years: the Holocene—a period of climate stability in which 'civilization' arose (Brown 2015).

Important indicators show that the *state of the Earth* (the sum of our planet's interacting physical, chemical, biological and human processes) has *drastically worsened* over the last 50–60 years. One set of global indicators studied by the Stockholm Resilience Center, which includes both socio-economic metrics (such as population, real GDP, foreign direct investment, the urban population, primary energy use, fertilizer consumption, water use, paper production, transportation, telecommunications and international tourism) and Earth System indicators (such as carbon dioxide, nitrous oxide, methane, surface temperature, ocean acidification, marine fish capture, tropical forest loss, domesticated land and degradation of terrestrial biosphere) clearly indicates the decline in sustainability since the 1950s (IGBP 2015).

In more detail, some attributes of the Anthropocene are completely new and can be observed in stratigraphic records. They include the following (Waters et al. 2016):

- the presence of new anthropogenic materials, including concrete, plastics and aluminum;
- the modification of more than 50% of Earth's land surface for human use. This also greatly impacts the health of oceans;
- the massive impact of human processes on nitrogen, phosphorus and carbon cycles;
- the impressive increase in average global sea levels (Waters et al. 2016);
- the accelerating loss of biodiversity and other biotic changes, including the worldwide spread of invasive species; and
- pervasive global fallout from nuclear weapons testing.

Using a 'planetary boundary' framework to define a 'safe operating space' for humanity, Steffen et al. (2015) show how the level of human perturbation of four Earth System processes/features (climate change, biosphere integrity, biogeochemical flows and land-system change) is exceeding safe limits.

5.2 Integral Ecology

The encyclical letter of Pope Francis (2015), *Praise Be to You: On Care for Our Common Home* (*Laudato si'*), represents an excellent opportunity to build a conversation between ethics, economics and ecology about sustainable development.

The encyclical underlines the human origins of the ecological crisis and proposes fundamental changes in terms of how economic and social life is organized. Important suggestions by the Pope include encouraging *frugality* of consumption and acknowledging the *intrinsic value of nature*. Adopting these suggestions poses a serious challenge to economics in general, and business in particular.

The encyclical criticizes the throwaway culture, which "generates so much waste, because of the disordered desire to consume more than what is really necessary" (Pope Francis 2015, para 123). It urges individuals to "modify [. . .] consumption, develop [. . .] an economy of waste disposal and recycling, protect [. . .] certain species and plan [. . .] a diversified agriculture and the rotation of crops" (ibid., para 180).

The Pope is concerned that "We have too many means and only a few insubstantial ends" (ibid., para 203). He encourages people to develop "more sober lifestyles, while reducing their energy consumption and improving its efficiency" (ibid., para 193) and believes that "a decrease in the pace of production and consumption can at times give rise to another form of progress and development" (ibid., para 191).

The encyclical underlines the fact that Christian spirituality proposes

> an alternative understanding of the quality of life, and encourages a prophetic and contemplative lifestyle, one capable of deep enjoyment free of the obsession with consumption. . . . We need to take up an ancient lesson, found in different religious traditions and also in the Bible. It is the conviction that "less is more."
>
> (ibid., para 222)

This involves a return to simplicity "which allows us to stop and appreciate the small things, to be grateful for the opportunities which life affords us, to be spiritually detached from what we possess, and not to succumb to sadness for what we lack" (ibid., para 222). "Happiness means knowing how to limit some needs" (ibid., para 223).

Today the most advanced economies overshoot ecological limits in a massive way (i.e., use many more environmental resources and space than their 'fair share'). Herman Daly (2008) has argued that, to encourage sustainability, frugality should precede efficiency as a priority. Making efficiency improvements alone is not adequate to reduce the material demand of our overgrown economies.

> An improvement in efficiency by itself is equivalent to having a larger supply of the factor whose efficiency increased. More uses of the cheaper factor will be found. We will end up consuming more of the resource than before, albeit more efficiently. Scale continues to grow.
>
> (Daly 2008: 222)

Frugality implies rebalancing material and spiritual values in economic life (Bouckaert et al. (Eds.) 2008). This may lead to the rehabilitation of the substantive meaning of 'economics' and the revival of the corresponding logic of sufficiency.

Thomas Princen (2005) argues that we need to move away from an economy built on the principles of profit maximization and efficiency to a logic of *sufficiency*. I agree with this position, and think that becoming more frugal "requires more substantive organizational forms that radically alter the underlying structure of currently dominating configurations of formal economizing. This means [. . .] introducing smaller scale, locally adaptable, culturally diverse mode of substantive economic activities" (Zsolnai 2002: 661).

Pope Francis urges us to accept the intrinsic value of nature and to express appreciation for it. Natural beings and ecosystems "have an intrinsic value independent of their usefulness. Each organism, as a creature of God, is good and admirable in itself; the same is true of the harmonious ensemble of organisms existing in a defined space and functioning as a system" (Pope Francis 2015, para 140).

The encyclical emphasizes that "environmental protection cannot be assured solely on the basis of financial calculations of costs and benefits. The environment is one of those goods that cannot be adequately safeguarded or promoted by market forces" (ibid., para 190).

Mainstream economics does not acknowledge the intrinsic value of nature. It promotes the evaluation of environmental goods and services on the basis of their *market value*, which is determined by competing economic actors. The value of components of nature is calculated by using the 'willingness to pay' principle, or shadow pricing techniques.

Ecological economics speaks about nature in terms of material-energy throughput and ecosystem services. This approach also appears to be problematic. Peter Brown (2015) argues that it is better to think about nature as the "commonwealth of life," appreciating the uniqueness and interconnectedness of all life forms on Earth.

Joan Martínez-Alier and others suggest that ecological economics should rest on the assumption of the weak comparability of values, which implies that there is no algorithmic solution to environmental (or other economic) decision problems (Martínez-Alier et al. 1998, Martínez-Alier and Muradian (Eds.) 2015).

One major attempt to integrate beauty and nature into modern science was made by Gregory Bateson (1972, 1979) who suggested that we can recover *grace* by realizing the nature of our interrelated membership in the community of living organisms on the planet.

> The route to this realization is personal engagement with the more-than-rational processes of the natural world and of human art. Poetry, painting, dance, music, humor, metaphor, the best of religion, and natural history, offer possibilities to a renewed access to wisdom that we accumulated during million of years of our evolution.
>
> (Charlton 2008: 152)

Sustainable development calls for the integration of science with the arts to promote more active engagement with the processes of living nature. By recognizing beauty in the world, we can more easily identify sane and health-giving opportunities for action.

The fact that 'nature is prior to us' is the common underlying message of all faith traditions and of most contemporary sciences, including physics, evolutionary psychology, ecology and systems theory. The main task now is to incorporate nature as a primordial stakeholder into the functioning of human organizations, including businesses, public administration and civil society organizations. The crucial question concerns how to develop the ecological sensitivity and responsiveness of people at different levels of organizations, and how then to translate the emerging ecological consciousness into effective and caring organizational practices that will help organizations develop a culture of Earth Citizenship (Brown 2015).

References

Bateson, G. 1972: *Steps to an Ecology of Mind: Collected Essays in Anthropology, Psychiatry, Evolution, and Epistemology*. Chicago: University of Chicago Press.

Bateson, G. 1979: *Mind and Nature: A Necessary Unity*. New York: Hampton Press.

Bouckaert, L., Opdebeeck, H. and Zsolnai, L. (Eds.) 2008: *Frugality: Rebalancing Material and Spiritual Values in Economic Life*. Oxford: Peter Lang Publishing.

Brown, P. G. 2015: "Ethics for Economics in the Anthropocene" in Brown, P. G. and Timmerman, Peter (Eds.): *Ecological Economics for the Anthropocene: An Emerging Paradigm*. New York: Columbia University Press. pp. 66–88.

Charlton, N. G. 2008: *Understanding Gregory Bateson: Mind, Beauty, and the Sacred Earth*. Albany: SUNY Press.

Crutzen, P. J. 2002: "Geology of Mankind" *Nature* Vol. 415, No. 3, January, p. 2.

Daly, H. 2008: "Frugality First" in Bouckaert, L., Opdebeeck, H. and Zsolnai, L. (Eds.): *Frugality: Rebalancing Material and Spiritual Values in Economic Life*. Oxford: Peter Lang Publishing. pp. 207–226.

IGBP, 2015: *The Great Acceleration*. www.stockholmresilience.org/21/research/research-news/1-15-2015-new-planetary-dashboard-shows-increasing-human-impact.html

Martínez-Alier, J. and Muradian, R. (Eds.) 2015: *Handbook of Ecological Economics*. Cheltenham: Edward Elgar.

Martínez-Alier, J., Munda, G. and O'Neill, J. 1998: "Weak Comparability of Values as a Foundation for Ecological Economics" *Ecological Economics* Vol. 26, pp. 277–286.

Orr, D. W. (2016): *Dangerous Years: Climate Change, the Long Emergency and the Way Forward*. New Haven and London: Yale University Press.

Pope Francis 2015: *Praise Be to You: On Care for Our Common Home*. Encyclical Letter *Laudatio Si'* of the Holy Father Francis. The Vatican City.

Princen, T. 2005: *The Logic of Sufficiency*. Boston: MIT Press.

Steffen, W., Persson, A., Deutsch, L., Zalasiewicz, J., Williams, M., Richardson, K., . . . Svedin, P. 2011: "The Anthropocene: From Global Change to Planetary Stewardship" *AMBIO* Vol. 40, pp. 739–761.

Steffen, W., Richardson, K., Rockström, J., Cornell, S. E., Fetzer, I., Bennett, E. M., . . . Sörlin, S. 2015: "Planetary Boundaries: Guiding Human Development on a Changing Planet" *Science* Vol. 347, No. 6223, p. 736 and 1259855–1–10.

Waters, C. N., Zalasiewicz, J., Summerhayes, C., Barnosky, A. D., Poirier, C., Gałuszka, A., and Wolfe, A. P. 2016: "The Anthropocene Is Functionally and Stratigraphically Distinct from the Holocene" *Science* Vol. 351, No. 6269, p. 137 and aad2622–1–10.

Zsolnai, L. 2002: "Green Business or Community Economy?" *International Journal of Social Economics* Vol. 29, No. 8, pp. 652–662.

6 Nurturing Place*

Not only is the market economy as a whole disembedded from society and nature (Polanyi 1944), but modern organizations, communities and people are also *disembedded* from the *environmental* and *social context* in which they operate. Modern business organizations, especially corporations, are rootless in an ecological and social sense and display strong disinterest in the places in which they function (Schumacher 1971).

6.1 Modern Business Organizations

Modern business organizations consider the natural environment and human persons as mere tools for accomplishing their narrowly defined purposes and goals. Their dominating self-centered orientation leads to decision paralysis that produces ecological and social destruction on a large scale. The perverse nature of the decisions made by modern business organizations is visible in phenomena such as decision-making under risk and discounting in space and time. Prospect theory and the general theory of discounting can help us to describe and analyze these phenomena (Zsolnai 2002).

To understand this type of perverse decision-making, we can turn to prospect theory. Prospect theory states that the majority of decision-makers prefer sure but smaller gains over greater but uncertain gains (i.e., decision-makers are usually risk averse in choices involving sure gains) (Kahneman and Tversky 1979). Moreover, a majority of decision-makers prefer to suffer greater but uncertain losses than smaller but certain losses. Decision-makers are usually risk-seeking in choices involving sure losses (ibid.).

Further, prospect theory predicts that the majority of decision-makers will prefer smaller but certain gains and greater but uncertain losses over smaller

*This chapter was written with Paul Shrivastava (Penn State University). An earlier version was presented at the Karl Polanyi International Conference in November 2014 in Montreal.

but certain losses and greater but uncertain gains. This is because decision-makers are more sensitive to losses than to gains (ibid.).

Risky decisions made by modern business organizations often endanger the long-term safety and integrity of the natural environment and human populations. So-called catastrophic risk is a case in point. The probability of the occurrence of a catastrophe caused by modern, large-scale technologies is usually low, but it is never zero. Yet the potentially negative consequences (losses) can be horrifying, including the destruction of ecosystems and enormous losses to society. Recent examples of these kinds of ecological and human tragedies include the Fukushima Nuclear Plant accident, the Bhopal disaster, and the BP oil spill in the Mexican gulf.

Decision-makers usually over-value things that are in the here and now compared to things that are further away and/or later in time. This phenomenon is called 'discounting.' The majority of decision-makers prefer to make gains here and now rather than to make the same gains further away and later in time. Decision-makers discount gains that are distant in space and time.

This decision logic underlies the increasing corporate institutional neglect of society and ecology, and the disembedding of companies.

Decision-makers tend to use discount rates to value things distant in space and time. If the distance of a thing in space or/and in time is great enough, then its present value becomes extremely small. Also, the present value depends on the discount rate that is applied: the greater the discount rate, the smaller the present value. The present value of a thing is thus determined by the discount rate and its distance in space and time. If the present generation wished to take into account the needs of two generations in the future and to protect the ecosystem health and the cultural heritage of mankind for three generations—say, 120 years hence—then an extremely low or even a negative discount rate would be needed.

Applying the 'normal' discount rate of 2–5% in business decision-making may increase disembedding. Decision-makers who strongly discount things in space and time are neither interested in solving long-term (or distant) ecological and human problems, nor in considering the global impacts of their activities on the natural environment and human communities. The international trade in hazardous wastes is an illustrative case in point. Developed countries transport and dump hazardous wastes in distant and less-developed countries, and do not display much interest in the ecological human health impacts of these materials. Another example is the ultra-low wages of tea plantation workers in India, or other farm laborers who are sometimes paid less than $1.25 per day.

By combining the main lessons of prospect theory and the general theory of discounting we obtain insight into the disembedding of modern business organizations from society and nature.

Let us consider the following decision-related problem. There are two alternatives available to a modern business organization. The first is to make a sure gain (G) here and now and a loss of yL at some point further away/later in time with a probability of $1/y$, where $y > 1$. The second alternative is to make a sure loss (L) here and now, and a gain of xG at some point further away/later in time with a probability of $1/x$, where $x > 1$.

Modern business organizations typically prefer the first alternative (to make smaller but sure gains here and now, and greater but uncertain losses further away/later in time) to the second one (greater but unsure gains here and now, and smaller but certain losses further away/later in time) (Table 6.1). This means that modern business organizations are likely to be engaged in fostering activity that supports here and now options; they may be studying them, devoting power to them, building relationships with them, and advocating or lobbying for them. Similarly, modern business organizations are liable to be disengaged with outcomes that are further away and later in time; the tendency is to deny their existence, lobby against them or maintain a position of silence about them.

Table 6.1 Self-Centered Choices of Modern Business Organizations

	Certain, here and now	*Uncertain, further and later*
Gains	**favor**	avoid
Losses	avoid	**favor**

The presented simplified model illustrates the dynamics of disembeddedness at the micro-level in the capitalist economy. The self-centered orientation of businesses leads to the development of disinterest in the environmental and social consequences of activities and policies, leading to functioning that is socially and environmentally disembedded and, ultimately, fuels the self-centeredness of modern-day businesses.

6.2 A Place-Based Approach to Sustainability

One potential solution for this tendency to disembedding is to employ a place-based approach to organizing. Shrivastava and Kennelly (2013) argue that without *respecting* and *nurturing* '*place*,' ecological sustainability cannot be fostered. Because 'genius loci' has an undeniable spiritual component, place-based enterprises cannot be run on a purely materialistic basis. The non-materialistic elements of place (such as aesthetics, cultural heritage, community feelings and transcendence) should be integrated into place-based management.

A passion for sustainability can override an appetite for material gains (Shrivastava 2010). Place-based enterprises are promising models in which the true meaning of *oikonomia* can be realized: support for livelihoods and the cultivation of the richness of nature.

Functioning according to a place-based approach can bring the following benefits to organizations: (i) managers who are dedicated to respecting and nurturing place may be strongly supported by local communities, (ii) employees may be morally satisfied and thus better motivated by serving the place in which they live and with which they identify, (iii) more high quality, environmentally minded employees can be recruited, (iv) customer loyalty can be strengthened and (v) trust-based relationships with local subcontractors and partners can be established.

The focus on place can also be a source of natural-resources-related benefits. For example, the qualities of soil, water, microclimate and vegetation create a unique 'terroir' through which many products (such as wine, cheese and agricultural produce) can be distinguished. For example, the domain of production of French wines is strictly regulated and a prized asset. The focus on place may also lend cultural advantages to enterprises in the form of labor practices and skills, the stronger value orientation of workers, increased public loyalty and social goodwill. Communities sometimes 'adopt' local companies as part of their extended families, and are willing to help them in times of economic and political uncertainty. In this way, placed-based, caring organizations are rewarded for their environmentally and socially responsible behavior by their heightened ability to generate commitment from managers, employees and the local community, and establish trust-based relationships with customers, subcontractors and other partners.

The following section illustrates the concept of the place-based sustainability framework using examples of re-embedding from Italy (Slow Food) and Japan (Echigo-Tsumari community development).

6.3 Slow Food

The *Arci Gola* (later, Arcigola) association was established in Italy by Carlo Petrini in 1986 to promote a gastronomic culture that combines the pleasure of food (and wine) with knowledge about local traditions, capabilities and the resources needed to create quality products (Petrini and Padovani 2005: 64–68). To advance an alternative to the prevailing, homogenizing, competitive model of business based on mass production, economic efficiency, standardization and fast food, Petrini and his friends decided to extend and further develop the Arcigola experience. Thus, in 1989 the *Slow Food* international association was launched in Paris by 400 members from 18 countries (ibid.: 97–101).

Today, Slow Food is a global, nonprofit, member-supported organization that has over 100,000 members. The goal of Slow Food is to implement a concept called neo-gastronomy. This innovative approach calls for an awareness of the cultural, historical, social and ecological conditions and processes that support the creation of quality food (Petrini 2005). Members believe that real gastronomic pleasure is combined with responsibility and care; that is, knowledge of and respect for local traditions, land, and cultural and biological diversity. Eco-gastronomy recognizes the strategic linkages among people, planet and plate. Creating local and sustainable food is the way to feed individuals while still respecting the carrying capacity of the Earth, and ensuring better living conditions for farmers and consumers.

This holistic perspective sees the quality of food as being deeply rooted in the quality of surrounding ecosystems; the material and non-material identity of local communities involved in cultivation, breeding, and production processes; and overall quality of life. Conviviality is based on the concepts of sharing and reciprocity. The pleasure of food should be shared, and dining is mainly seen as an expression of sociality. Thus, Slow Food promotes food and wine culture by defending and safeguarding the cultural heritage of local communities, the social relationships that express them, and interconnected biodiversity.

The idea of quality fostered by Slow Food encompasses three principles (Petrini 2005, Slow Food International 2011):

(i)   Food must be good—meaning that food should taste good and give pleasure according to the criteria of authenticity and naturalness, as relevant to certain moments, specific places and within defined cultures.

(ii) Food must be clean—produced in a sustainable way that does not harm the environment, damage animal welfare or degrade human health. With regard to this goal, traditional production practices are favored, as they have less negative ecological and social impacts, and also help to restore and protect ecosystems and ecosystems services.

(iii) Food must be fair—meaning that producers should receive fair compensation for the work they do; should work under humane conditions; and their dignity, knowledge and capabilities should be valued and respected.

This approach to quality requires alternative and innovative means of production and consumption, which are in contrast with the mainstream practices of large-scale agribusiness. It is based on three pillars (Tasch 2008): (i) *small*, the adoption of an appropriate scale in social, environmental and economic terms; (ii) *local*, being respectful of and embedded in the natural environment and community; and (iii) *slow*, because the creation of quality products takes time and passion, and a slow approach is crucial for promoting a more responsible, just and caring way of living, in line with natural and human rhythms.

To foster this agenda, Slow Food aims to:

- Educate consumers. If the goal is to change the way food is produced and consumed, and more generally, the way people live, education is critical. Eating is a political act that requires making informed choices. Therefore, passive consumers must become active and aware co-producers who appreciate and choose to consume quality food and support more sustainable agricultural practices.
- Connect producers and co-producers to build opportunities for exchange and to foster a virtuous cycle that promotes the creation of excellent products and overcomes the constraints of currently dominant mass food production techniques.
- Protect biodiversity, not only of fruit, vegetables and animal species, but also of local customs and traditions that make food and life pleasant and fitting.

To meet these goals, Slow Food develops projects that are engines of innovation and help disseminate best advanced practice. These include the University of Gastronomic Sciences (UNISG), Salone Internazionale del Gusto (International Fair of Taste), and the Slow Food Foundation for Biodiversity.

In connection with Slow Food, the *Slow Cities International* movement was established in Orvieto, Italy, in 1999. The movement's underlying philosophy is that alternative patterns of development can be created only by starting at the local community scale, and, in particular, in towns and cities with fewer than 50,000 inhabitants where living a slow life is still possible, and in which landscape, culture, memories and traditions are still respected and fostered. Thus, the label *Cittaslow* has become the mark of quality for small, high-quality municipalities that decide to join the association through making specific commitments to improving the quality of life of inhabitants.

The Cittaslow movement has expanded to 236 cities in 30 countries across the world (including many European countries and Australia, Canada, China, New Zealand, South Africa, South Korea and the United States), connecting municipalities, citizens and Slow Food partners (Cittaslow International 2017).

6.4 Arts-Based Community Regeneration

A special case of organizational embedding is the *Echigo-Tsumari Art Field* (ETAF) initiative in the Nigata region of Japan. This venture has the goal of regenerating the biologically, socially and culturally rich nature of *satoyama* existence in the Echigo-Tsumari region. This part of Japan has been devastated by young people leaving village communities to make their lives in urban cities, with consequent abandonment of farming practices and bio-diversity loss. The ETAF project uses art to recover memories of place and restore natural environments. This is the origin of the concept "humans are part of nature," which has become the overarching principle for the entire Echigo-Tsumari Art Field movement. Regional development in Echigo-Tsumari is promoted by creating a model showing how people can relate to nature.

Echigo-Tsumari is known for heavy snowfall in winter. This motivates cultural exchange based upon the principle captured in the Japanese expression *seikô udoku; kakô tôdoku*, which can be rendered in English as "In summer, cultivate the fields; in winter, cultivate the mind." Cultural facilities, created by international artists and maintained by local people, warmly welcome visitors and travelers. To view artworks, visitors pass through terraced rice fields and forests of native beech, encountering festivals and traditional customs and experiencing the landscapes and cultures of Echigo-Tsumari through all five senses. Through this experience, visitors recover the memories of their origins that they may have forgotten, and develop new connections to others and to the land.

The nature and lifestyle of the satoyama of Echigo-Tsumari environment inspires artists to recover the connections and forms of collaboration that art once fostered, but which have almost been lost. Artworks are dotted across approximately 200 villages rather than displayed in a single center, an "absolutely inefficient" approach deliberately at odds with the trend towards the rationalization and efficiency of modern society. Wandering among these artworks, which emphasize the beauty and richness of satoyama and reveal the temporally accumulated layers of human inhabitation, opens the senses to the wonder of existence and revives the soul.

Approximately 160 artworks by artists from around the world are dotted across the 760 square kilometers of the Echigo-Tsumari Art Field. Satoyama can be felt and discovered in different seasons via these artworks located in fields, unoccupied houses and closed schools.

In Echigo-Tsumari, artists have no choice but to create their artwork on someone else's land, requiring interaction with locals. The artists' passion and openness to learning moves local people who then engage with the artwork not as spectators but as collaborators.

The Echigo-Tsumari Art Triennial has welcomed many young volunteers from cities. These individuals are known as the *kohebi-tai* (little shrimp gang) and have been involved in many different projects. The encounters between the elderly inhabitants who have spent their entire lives farming thinly populated lands and students who lack clear purpose in their city lives at first resulted in collision and confusion, but this has since been transformed into an attitude of appreciation and cooperation, leading to the opening up of the region.

It was artists and these city-based supporters who became actively engaged in supporting the area after the Chuetsu earthquake in 2004 and the heavy snowfall of two winters under the auspices of the *Daichi no otetsudai* (Help the Land) project which involved activities such as reconstruction work and snow removal. Through such work, it became apparent that Echigo-Tsumari represented a place for hope for those living in the cities. Young people, as well as those with more experience, are working together to build a 'new hometown.'

The way in which Echigo-Tsumari has succeeded in community building has been acknowledged outside the world of art by the *Furusato Event Award* (presented by the Ministry of Internal Affairs), the *Tokyo Creation Award* and the *Machi-tsukuri Commendation* by the General Affairs Minister, among other awards. The approach to community building through culture and art has drawn significant attention to the role of the area as a type of 'creative city,' and Echigo-Tsumari has influenced other community building projects in Tokushima, Ibaraki, Niigata, Osaka and Setouchi.

In addition to the Triennial itself, visitors can enjoy the Summer Festival (*Daichi-no-matsuri*) and the winter *Snow Art Project*, which coincide with local festivals and traditional events that are held throughout the year. Daichi-no-matsuri takes place in the years between the Triennial, welcoming visitors and displaying artwork to the public.

Major facilities, such as Matsudai Nohbutai and Kyororo, and the artworks in unoccupied houses and abandoned schools are a part of public programs through which one can learn about and experience local life, culture and science throughout the year. Training programs are also organized for schools and companies.

Performances and entertainment from all over the world are presented on the unique stage of Echigo-Tsumari, set amongst artworks and terraced rice fields.

6.5 Implications

What is common to the two organizations just described is a deep respect for nature and communities. The mainstream model of business can be compared with the place-based model (Table 6.2). Mainstream businesses base their functioning on the principle of self-interest, while their main goal is to maximize profit, or shareholder value. Their criterion of success is growth, measured in monetary terms. The typical form of ownership is corporate, while governance structures are generally hierarchical and non-participative.

Table 6.2 Competitive Versus Place-Based Organizations

	Competitive model	*Place-based model*
Basic motive	Self-interest	Care for place and inhabitants
Main goal	Maximize profit or shareholder value	Respect and nurture place, create value for all stakeholders
Criterion of success	Growth in monetary terms	Maintenance of natural wealth and social cohesion
Ownership	Corporate or private	Cooperative or individual
Governance	Hierarchical, non-participative	Democratic, participative

In contrast, place-based organizations respect and nurture the place in which they operate, and aim to create value for all stakeholders. Their criteria for success are the maintenance of natural wealth and an increase in social cohesion. Ownership forms are cooperative or individual, while their governance structure is democratic and participative.

'Place' should not be considered an accidental and external factor for organizations, communities and individuals. The fostering of linkages and practices with the 'spirit of place' can inspire individuals and organizations to find meaning, identity and a means of flourishing in a historical and ecological context.

References

Cittaslow International 2017: www.cittaslow.net/ (Accessed on October 16, 2017).

Kahneman, D. and Tversky A. 1979: "Prospect Theory: An Analysis of Decision Under Risk" *Econometrica* March, pp. 263–291.

Petrini, C. 2005: Buono, Pulito e Giusto. *Principi di Nuova Gastronomia*. Einaudi, Turin.

Petrini, C. and Padovani, G. 2005: *Slow Food Revolution. Da Arcigola a Terra Madre. Una Nuova Cultura del Cibo e della Vita*. Milan: Rizzoli.

Polanyi, K. 1944: *The Great Transformation*. Boston: Beacon Press.

Schumacher, E. F. 1971: *Small Is Beautiful*. London: Abacus.

Shrivastava, P. 2010: "Pedagogy of Passion for Sustainability" *Academy of Management Learning & Education* Vol. 9, No. 3, pp. 443–455.

Shrivastava, P. and Kennelly, J. J. 2013: "Sustainability and Place-Based Enterprise" *Organization & Environment* Vol. 26, No. 1, pp. 83–101.

Slow Food International 2011: www.slowfood.com/ (Accessed on December 14, 2011).

Tasch, W. 2008: *Inquiries into the Nature of Slow Money: Investing as if Food, Farms, and Fertility Mattered*. White River Junction, VT: Chelsea Green Publishing Company.

Tencati, A. and Zsolnai, L. 2010: "The Collaborative Enterprise Framework" in Tencati, A. and Zsolnai, L. (Eds.): *The Collaborative Enterprise: Creating Values for a Sustainable World*. Oxford: Peter Lang Academic Publishers. pp. 3–14.

Zsolnai, L. 2002: "Green Business or Community Economy?" *International Journal of Social Economics* Vol. 29, No. 8, pp. 652–662.

7 The Fate of Future Generations

In today's rapidly changing and interconnected world, numerous decisions that humans make will impact the fate and quality of life of people yet to be born. Consequently, *future generations* have a stake in the present functioning of business and society. The imperative of responsibility suggests that organizations, communities and people have a non-reciprocal duty to care for future generations.

Businesses create wealth without considering the impact of their activity on people yet to be born. The unintended consequence of these business decisions is 'illth' for future generations, especially when such activities transgress the ecologically safe limits of the biosphere and contribute to the destruction of the culture of local communities (Daly 2005). Examples of such activities include making decisions that will have an impact more than one life time in the future, creating and using technology with unknown risks, and causing widespread, uncontrollable changes to Earth's biogeochemical system.

7.1 The Moral Status of Future Generations

Hans Jonas has argued that the ethics of responsibility involve not only the existence of future human beings, but also the way in which they exist. The conditions in which future generations live should not significantly reduce their freedom and humanity.

> Thus moral responsibility demands that we take into consideration the welfare of those who, without being consulted, will later be affected by what we are doing now. Without our choosing it, responsibility becomes our lot due to the sheer extent of the power we exercise daily.
>
> (Jonas 1996: 99)

In his opus magnum, *The Imperative of Responsibility: In Search of an Ethics for the Technological Age*, Hans Jonas describes the impact of modern technology on the human condition (Jonas 1984). His theses are as follows:

(1) The nature of human activities has been altered and enlarged due to their magnitude and novelty, and their impact on man's global future.

(2) Responsibility is correlated to power, and must be commensurate with the latter's scope and its exercise.

(3) To replace the former projections of hope, an imaginative 'heuristics of fear' should be developed to inform us of what may be at stake, and what we must beware of.

(4) Ethics are created and underpinned by how man perceives his duties towards himself, his distant posterity, and the plenitude of life under his dominion.

(Jonas 1984: x)

Jonas argues that an imperative of responsibility might be framed like this: "Act so that the effects of your action are compatible with the permanence of genuine human life." Or, expressed negatively: "Act so that the effects of your action are not destructive of the future possibility of such life" (Jonas 1984: 11).

Prospective responsibility is never formal, but always substantive. It involves humans being responsible not primarily for their own conduct and its consequences, but for the matter that has or will make a claim on present action. The well-being, the interests, the fates of others have, by circumstance or by agreement, come to our care, which means that our control over them involves at the same time our obligation towards them (Jonas 1984: 92–93).

Jonas suggests differentiating between natural responsibility and contractual responsibility:

> It is the distinction between natural responsibility, where the immanent 'ought-to-be' of the object claims its agent a priori and quite unilaterally, and contracted or appointed responsibility, which is conditional a posteriori upon the fact and the terms of the relationship actually entered into.
>
> (Jonas 1984: 95)

The sustainable development discourse routinely makes references to the Brundtland Committee definition of sustainability, which states that "Sustainable development is development that meets the needs of the present without compromising the ability of future generations to meet their own needs" (Our

Common Future 1987: 43). However, this definition is usually used only in lip service to sustainability. In many cases, corporate sustainability is defined and measured without consideration of the impact of corporate functioning on the fate and living standards of future generations.

In the business ethics literature, Jeurissen and Keijzers (2004) argue that the obligation of business to future generations should be established on the basis of the theories of rights, utilitarianism and justice. Rights theory suggests that even though future generations do not yet exist, they have a moral right to have a livable environment. Utilitarianism tells us that we should take future generations into account because of their happiness and their vulnerability, and requires that we should seek to promote the best existence for all generations. Finally, theories about justice require that every generation should reserve a portion of its wealth for the sake of future generations.

Arenas and Ridrigo (2013) criticize the concept of future generations as an abstract and vague construct, arguing that businesses have only a 'thin' (minimal and impartial) responsibility toward future generations that is based on the principle of benevolence. For this reason, they do not support the idea that future generations should be acknowledged as stakeholders of firms.

The Blueprint for Better Business suggests that businesses should serve as the guardians of future generations, and has developed the following criteria for 'high purpose' businesses. Such businesses (i) honor their duty to protect the natural world and conserve finite resources, (ii) contribute knowledge and experience to promote better regulation for the benefit of society as a whole rather than protecting their self-interest and (iii) invest in developing skills, knowledge and understanding in society to encourage informed citizenship (Blueprint 2015).

7.2 The Case of Seventh Generation, Inc.

Since the impact of modern business organizations are widespread and far-reaching, their responsibility also extends beyond meeting the perceived interests of a narrow set of stakeholders. Future generations should be considered stakeholders of business, and be included on the list of parties whose interests should be taken seriously.

Deliberate, systematic consideration of the interests of future generations is a rare phenomenon in today's business practice, but there are exceptional companies that strive to incorporate such concerns into their operations. One such company is *Seventh Generation, Inc.*, located in the USA.

Jeffrey Hollender is a leading authority on corporate responsibility, sustainability and social equity in the USA. He co-founded Seventh Generation,

Inc., and transformed it from a fledgling company into a leading brand of natural products known for its authenticity, transparency and progressive business practices. Although Hollander left the company in 2010, Seventh Generation continues to follow its noble purpose and mission.

Seventh Generation Inc. articulates a commitment to go beyond producing cleaner and greener products. It wants to create cultural changes and to shape consumer behavior and business ethics. Living up to its name (taken from the *Great Iroquois Law* that prescribes deliberation of the impact of all of our activities on the next seven generations), the novel formulas of the company's household and personal care products ensure that consumers can make a difference through keeping toxic material out of the environment, preserving natural resources and reducing pollution.

The company's products are manufactured in the most sustainable way possible. The ingredients used in products such as dishwashing liquids, laundry detergents, household cleaners and feminine care items are safe for the environment and do not create health risks. Paper products are made using only recycled, bleach-free paper (World Inquiry's Innovation Bank 2015).

The company's environmental sensitivity is manifested in its product development standards, the kind of materials it uses, product transportation and other emissions-related activities, regulatory compliance, the lifecycle analysis approach, systems thinking and its employment of biomimicry in the design of products and packaging.

The company encourages consumers to get involved in their efforts to save the planet. Green tips, ideas for better products and reviews of existing products are proactively sought from customers through the company's website. The organization's newsletter helps consumers make informed choices and raises environmental awareness.

The company has also launched an innovative program called 20/20. The objective of the initiative is to reduce greenhouse gas emissions by 20% through energy efficiency measures, and another 20% by using renewable energy. Implementation of the program involves the use of an open-source software tracker that allows employees to enter information about their monthly use of fossil energy. The system processes the data and calculates the user's carbon footprint using various visual outputs. The company also incentivizes employee participation.

Exhibiting corporate consciousness through its supply chain, the organization uses a report called a "Manufacturing Partner Annual Report" as a tool for evaluating suppliers in an integrated fashion. The appraisal criteria require the use of data about energy use, greenhouse gas generation and waste production.

The organization exists through its undying belief in the ability of commerce to re-make the world, and its espousal of a new corporate paradigm that is concerned with more than protecting the environment. It helps develop new markets, position more responsible products and brands in these markets, and attract a vibrant workforce that is committed to making a change. Through its innovative business practices, the company has created avenues for suppliers, partners, shareholders, customers and employees to express their idealism, passion and commitment to causes larger than themselves at every point in the value chain—truly making a difference one household cleaning spray at a time (World Inquiry's Innovation Bank 2015).

Table 7.1 summarizes the profile of the company.

Table 7.1 Main Characteristics of Seventh Generation, Inc.

	Seventh Generation, Inc.
Spiritual inspiration	Aboriginal ethics
Mission	Creating cultural change through shaping consumer behavior and business ethics
Core values	Authenticity, transparency, progressiveness
Business model	Providing natural household and personal care products
Environmental and/or social performance	Keeping toxic material out of the environment, preserving natural resources and reducing pollution
Stakeholder engagement	Green tips, ideas for better products and reviews of existing products are proactively sought out from customers through the company website

7.3 Assessment for Future Generations

How can we evaluate business activities from the perspective of future generations?

Edith Brown Weiss (1989) developed three principles, which specify our obligations to future generations:

(i)   Each generation should be required to conserve the diversity of the natural and cultural resource base so that it does not unduly restrict the options available to future generations for solving their problems. This principle is called the "conservation of options."

(ii)   Each generation should be required to maintain the quality of the planet so that it is passed on in no worse condition than the present generation received it. This principle is called the "conservation of quality."

(iii) Each generation should support the access of future generations to the legacy of past generations. This principle is called the "conservation of access."

The Stiglitz et al. report (2009) states that the notion of sustainability refers to the challenge of determining whether we can hope to see the current level of well-being at least maintained for future periods or future generations, or whether the most likely scenario is that it will decline. The idea is the following: the well-being of future generations compared to ours will depend on what resources we pass on to them. Many different types of resource may be included in this transfer. Future well-being will depend upon the magnitude of the stocks of exhaustible resources that current generations leave untouched, but also on how well we maintain the quantity and quality of all the other renewable natural resources that are necessary for life. From an economic perspective, it will also depend upon how much physical capital—machines, infrastructure, etc.—we pass on, and how much we devote to building the human capital of future generations, essentially through expenditure on education and research. It will also depend upon the quality of the institutions that we transmit to them, which represent another form of capital that is crucial to the maintenance of a properly functioning society (Stiglitz et al. 2009).

The question is how can we evaluate whether enough assets will remain (or be accumulated) for future generations? The Stiglitz et al. report (2009) suggests that we should use indicators to inform us about changes in the quantities of different resources that matter for future well-being. Put differently, sustainability requires the simultaneous preservation of, or increase in, several 'stocks' which include the quantity and quality of natural resources, and human, social and physical capital (ibid.: 17).

I agree with the argument that what will really matter for the well-being of future generations is what access they have to what quantities and qualities of different stocks or forms of capital. However, I think that *thresholds* should be defined for these stocks or capitals against which we can evaluate the current state of affairs (Zsolnai 2010).

Using this prospective system, if the state/quantity of a certain stock or capital falls below a defined threshold, this indicates that the present generation is creating a burden for future generations as regards that specific stock. Similarly, if the state of a certain stock or capital remains above (or is accumulated above) a defined threshold, then this will indicate that present generations have gifted future generations the quantity/quality of that stock. A stock's equivalence with a defined threshold will indicate that the impacts of present generations on future generations are neither negative nor positive in that area.

A company can be said to be future-oriented (i.e., respectful of the interests of future generations) if it contributes to the restoration and conservation of ecological capital, helps to maintain demographic health through the families of its employees, contributes fairly to the preservation of cultural heritage and invests adequately into research and development.

Accepting responsibility for future generations requires a *transformation of business*. Businesses should contribute to the conservation and restoration of nature, to the preservation of the culture of societies and to the development of new technologies in order to respect the interest of future generations (Zsolnai 2006).

Using financial and non-financial resources for the sake of future generations may seem to be rather idealistic. But caring for future generations need not only be done out of altruistic concern. A company's efforts to improve the position of future generations will also enhance the prospects of that company as well. Maintaining and developing ecological, social, cultural and intellectual capital creates strength in business organizations. Businesses that seek to sustain themselves in the long-term cannot avoid considering future generations as important stakeholders whose interests should be defined and served.

References

Arenas, D. and Ridrigo, P. 2013: "The Challenge of Future Generations for Business Ethics" *Journal of Management for Global Sustainability* Vol. 1, No. 1, pp. 47–69.

Blueprint 2015: *Blueprint for Better Business*. www.blueprintforbusiness.org/principles/ (Accessed on November 26, 2015).

Brown Weiss, E. 1989: *In Fairness to Future Generations: International Law, Common Patrimony, and Intergeneration Equity*. Tokyo: The United Nations University and Dobbs Ferry; New York: Transnational Publishers, Inc.

Daly, H. E. 2005: "Economics in a Full World" *Scientific American* September, pp. 100–107.

Jeurissen, R. and Keijzers, G. 2004: "Future Generations and Business Ethics" *Business Ethics Quarterly* Vol. 14, No. 1, pp. 47–69.

Jonas, H. 1984: *The Imperative of Responsibility: In Search of an Ethics for the Technological Age*. Chicago and London: University of Chicago Press.

Jonas, H. 1996: "Toward an Ontological Grounding of an Ethics for the Future" in Jonas, H. (Ed.): *Mortality and Morality. A Search for the Good After Auschwitz*. Evanston, IL: Northwestern University Press. pp. 99–112.

Our Common Future 1987: *Our Common Future—the Brundtland Report*. Oxford and New York: Oxford University Press.

Stiglitz, J., Sen, A. and Fitoussi, J-P. 2009: *Report by the Commission on the Measurement of Economic Performance and Social Progress*. www.stiglitz-sen-fitoussi. fr (Accessed on November 11, 2015).

World Inquiry's Innovation Bank 2015: *Seventh Generation—Preserving the Planet for Next Seven Generations and Beyond*. https://worldinquiry.case.edu/bankInnov ationView?idArchive=640 (Accessed on November 29, 2015).

Zsolnai, L. 2006: "Extended Stakeholder Theory" *Society and Business Review* Vol. 1, No. 1, pp. 37–44.

Zsolnai, L. 2010: "Respect for Future Generations" in Bouckaert, L. and Arena, P. (Eds.): *Respect and Economic Democracy*. Antwerp and Appeldom: Garant. pp. 29–36.

Part IV

Business and Economics

8   The Fallacy of Stakeholder Management

Modern business has a widespread impact on the fate and survival of natural ecosystems and the living conditions of present and future generations. To meet its general responsibilities, business should undergo deep transformation so that it functions in a sustainable, pro-social and future-respecting way.

8.1 Maurice Clark Revisited

One hundred years ago, J. Maurice Clark—an eminent economist at the University of Chicago and Columbia University—published a paper entitled "The Changing Basis of Economic Responsibility" (Clark 1916). In this paper, Clark argues for a broadening of attitude toward the responsibilities entailed in business relationships, and states that the general responsibility of business is a fact.

Clark points out that we have inherited an economics of irresponsibility.

> We are in an economy of control with which our intellectual inheritance fits but awkwardly. To make control really tolerable we need something more; something which is still in its infancy. We need an economics of responsibility, developed and embodied in our working business ethics.
>
> (Clark 1916: 210)

Clark's claim is that we need all the sense of responsibility we can arouse. This is because

> We are coming to see that our everyday business dealings have more far-reaching effects than we have ever realized, and that the system of free contract is by itself quite inadequate to bring home the responsibility for these effects. We have begun to realize the many inappropriable values that are created and the many unpaid damages that are inflicted in the course of business exchanges.
>
> (Clark 1916: 217–218)

In Clark's view, "laissez-faire economics may well be characterized as the economics of irresponsibility, and the business system of free contract is also a system of irresponsibility when judged by the same standard" (Clark 1916: 218).

Clark emphasizes that every act has numberless effects on others.

> These by-products may often be far more important in the aggregate than the one service or the one sacrifice over which a voluntary bargain happens to be struck. [. . .] No one who appreciates this fact can hold that a system of free contract normally protects all interests, and that every free business transaction is automatically self-supporting and productive for society as a whole.
>
> (Clark 1916: 222)

The development of business and business ethics in the last 100 years has largely proved the truth of Clark's arguments.

Today's corporate transgressions are not exceptions, but everyday business phenomena. The numerous corporate scandals of the past two decades and the growing 'corporate criticism' literature illustrate this point well. While these accounts are sometimes accused of being selective in terms of cases and the presentation of anecdotal evidence, academics have provided a thorough and critical analysis of today's questionable business practices.

8.2 Limitations of the Stakeholder Management Paradigm

The stakeholder management paradigm has become a core pillar of business, providing management with a clear frame of reference with which to connect the domains of ethics and business. Stakeholder management is the suggested cure for the social, ethical and environmental malfunctioning of business.

Stakeholder theory (Freeman et al. 2010) says that businesses and other organizations should consider the interests and claims of stakeholders and manage their activities accordingly. According to this perspective, the effective management of stakeholders is a strategic activity that is necessary for success, as it generates value for shareholders and ensures the long-term survival and sustainability of an organization. Ignoring stakeholders is dangerous, not just because it is morally inappropriate but also because it does not make economic sense.

There are two interrelated problems with this approach: (i) the narrow conception of stakeholders and (ii) the fallibility of the stakeholders concerning their own well-being.

A company's set of stakeholders is usually defined in a narrow way. Only owners, managers, employees, creditors, suppliers and local communities are considered stakeholders of business. This narrow definition of stakeholders is often a recipe for disaster in terms of organizational functioning.

Mitroff (1998) argues that when stakeholders are defined too narrowly, and/or are not identified correctly, this leads to *solving the wrong problems precisely*. This is especially striking in new situations. When managers confront a problem that is located at the edge of their competence, especially a novel problem, or a case outside the bounds of accepted thinking and practice, they are either stymied to the point of paralysis, or fall back on the only resource they have: reducing a novel or unique situation to a problem that they already know how to solve.

> The trouble is that the problems that one knows how to solve may bear little resemblance to the actual problems one needs to solve. As a result, extreme cases and outlier problems and situations pose a real and a serious challenge to the professions and to accepted modes of thinking. In the extreme, they lead to serious errors, catastrophic failures, and major disasters and crises.
>
> (Mitroff and Silvers 2009: 29)

Systems theory suggests that the overall performance of an organization is determined by the adequacy of the basic assumptions on which it functions, and on the way the system is capable of pursuing its objectives. Problems indicate that the basic assumptions are inadequate and/or the system is incapable of performing adequately (Ackoff 2004).

Organizations should *dissolve* rather than solve problems by redesigning the relevant systems to eliminate problems and preclude their reappearance. Business leaders should conceptualize problems and opportunities within the largest possible context. They should take into account the effects of any proposed action on all of the relevant stakeholders. It is not enough to "do things right": business should also "do the right things" (Ims and Zsolnai 2009).

Psychology and behavioral economics have revealed the fact that people are rather poor at predicting their own future well-being. They are fallible in terms of understanding what they will like in the future, and how they will feel in future states of affairs.

Daniel Kahneman criticizes the rational choice model on the basis of experimental research findings that indicate that people are myopic in their decisions, lack skill at predicting their future tastes and can be led to making erroneous choices through their fallible memories and incorrect evaluations of past experiences (Kahneman 2011).

Kahneman suggests differentiating between experienced utility and predicted utility. The experienced utility of an outcome is a measure of the hedonic experience of that outcome. The predicted utility of an outcome is defined as the individual's beliefs about its experienced utility at some future time. Predicted utility is an ex-ante variable, while experienced utility is an ex-post variable in the decision-making process.

According to the rational choice model used in stakeholder theory, decisions are made on the basis of predicted utility. If experienced utility greatly differs from predicted utility then this may lead to sub-rational or even irrational choices. The problem of predicted utility raises the question "Do people know what they will like?" The answer is a definite "No." The accuracy of people's hedonic predictions is generally quite poor.

Experimental studies suggest two conclusions: (i) people may have little ability to forecast changes in their hedonic responses to stimuli and (ii) even in situations that permit accurate hedonic predictions, people may tend to make decisions about future consumption without due consideration of possible changes in their tastes (Kahneman 2011).

Discrepancies between *retrospective utility* and *real-time utility* should also be addressed. This leads to the question: "Do people know what they have liked?" The answer is again a definite "No." Psychological experiments show that retrospective evaluations should be viewed with greater distrust than introspective reports of current experience.

The results of these studies support the following two empirical generalizations: (i) the Peak and End Rule, that is, global evaluations are predicted with high accuracy by a weighted combination of the most extreme affect recorded during the episode and of the affect recorded during the terminal moments of the episode; (ii) Duration Neglect, that is, the retrospective evaluation of overall or total pain (or pleasure) is not affected by the period of duration (Kahneman 2011).

Since people use their evaluative memories to guide them in their choices about future outcomes, deceptive retrospective evaluations may lead to erroneous choices. Kahneman identifies two major obstacles to maximizing experienced utility. People lack skill at predicting how their tastes might change. It is difficult to describe as rational agents those individuals who are prone to making large errors in predicting what they will want or enjoy next week. Another obstacle is a tendency to use the affect associated with particular moments as a proxy for the utility of extended outcomes. Observations of memory biases are significant because the evaluation of the past determines what is learned from it. Errors in the lessons drawn from experience will inevitably be reflected in deficient choices for the future (Kahneman 2011).

Managing for a narrowly defined set of stakeholders cannot guarantee that whole ecosystems will be sustainable in an ecological sense, or beneficial for society at large, including future generations. Considering the interest of stakeholders solely on the basis of their own calculations may lead to sub-optimal outcomes. Business and other organizations should expand their set of stakeholders and look beyond their rationally calculated self-interests.

8.3 Primordial Stakeholders

Nature, society and future generations should be considered primordial stakeholders of organizations (Zsolnai 2006). We can evaluate the activities of organizations from the perspective of nature, from the perspective of society and from the perspective of future generations.

From the perspective of nature, *integrity* is a central value. The notion of ecological integrity was first introduced by the American naturalist Aldo Leopold in his environmental classic, *A Sand County Almanac*. He wrote: "A thing is right when it tends to preserve the integrity, stability, and beauty of the biotic community. It is wrong when it tends otherwise" (Leopold 1948: 225).

The activities of an organization can be evaluated against *sustainability indicators* that operationalize the notion of ecological integrity (Azar et al. 1996).

Let **A** be a specific activity of an organization. Let $E1, \ldots, Ei, \ldots, Em$ be sustainability indicators ($m > 1$).

$Ei(\ )$ is an ecological value function which is defined as follows:

$$(1) \quad Ei(A) = \begin{cases} 1 & \text{if activity } A \text{ is good regarding} \\ & \text{sustainability indicator } Ei; \\ 0 & \text{if activity } A \text{ is neutral regarding} \\ & \text{sustainability indicator } Ei; \\ -2 & \text{if activity } A \text{ is bad regarding} \\ & \text{sustainability indicator } Ei. \end{cases}$$

$Ei(A)$ reflects the ecological value of activity **A** regarding sustainability indicator **Ei**.

The following vector represents the ecological value of activity **A** regarding all the sustainability indicators $E1, \ldots, Ei, \ldots, Em$.

$$(2) \quad E(A) = [E1(A), \ldots, Ei(A), \ldots, Em(A)]$$

To obtain an aggregate picture about the ecological value of a certain activity, we should define weights that reflect the relative importance of the sustainability indicators. Let $w1, \ldots, wi, \ldots, wm$ be such weights.

It is required that:

(3) $\Sigma \, wi = 1$

The aggregate ecological value of activity **A** can be calculated as follows:

(4) $E(A) = \Sigma \, wi \, Ei(A)$

E(A) reflects the aggregate ecological value of activity **A** $(1 \geq E(A) \geq -2)$.

An activity can be considered *sustainable* if and only if its aggregate ecological value is positive. That is, if:

(5) $E(A) > 0$

Evaluating activity systems from a social perspective has been a long lasting enterprise of welfare economics. Here human well-being is the central value.

Amartya Sen proposed that human well-being should be understood in terms of *capabilities*. Capabilities are primarily a reflection of the freedom a person has to function in a valuable way, hence they can be interpreted as the substantive freedom that people enjoy (Sen 1992).

Let **C1**, . . . , **Cj**, . . . , **Cn** be capability indicators against which activity systems can be evaluated: $(j > 1)$

Let **Cj ()**—the social value function—be defined as follows:

$$
(6) \;\; Cj(A) =
\begin{cases}
1 & \text{if activity } \mathbf{A} \text{ is good regarding capability indicator } \mathbf{Cj}; \\
0 & \text{if activity } \mathbf{A} \text{ is neutral regarding capability indicator } \mathbf{Cj}; \\
-2 & \text{if activity } \mathbf{A} \text{ is bad regarding capability indicator } \mathbf{Cj}.
\end{cases}
$$

Cj(A) reflects the social value of activity **A** regarding capability indicator **Cj**.

The following vector represents the social value of activity **A** regarding all the capability indicators **C1**, . . . , **Cj**, . . . , **Cn**.

(7) $C(A) = [C1(A), \ldots, Cj(A), \ldots, Cn(A)]$

To obtain an aggregate picture about the social value of activity **A** we should introduce weights that reflect the relative importance of the capability indicators. Let **u1**, . . . , **uj**, . . . , **un** be such importance weights.

It is required that:

(8) $\Sigma \, uj = 1$

The aggregate social value of activity **A** can be calculated as follows:

(9) $C(A) = \Sigma \; uj \; Cj(A)$

C(A) reflects the aggregate social value of activity **A** $(1 \geq C(A) \geq -2)$

An activity can be considered *pro-social* if its aggregate social value is positive. That is, if:

(10) $C(A) > 0$

How can we evaluate a certain activity from the perspective of future generations? We cannot know too much about the needs of future generations, but freedom is sure to be of central importance.

As mentioned in Chapter 7, Edith Brown Weiss (1989) developed some criteria for assessing the freedom of future generations, namely: (i) conservation of options, (ii) conservation of quality and (iii) conservation of access.

Considering principles (i), (ii) and (iii), indicators for future generations can be generated. Let **F1, . . . , Fk, . . . , Fp** be the indicators against which activities can be evaluated: $(p > 1)$

The future generations' value function **Fk ()** is defined as follows:

$$
(11) \; \mathbf{Fk(A)} = \begin{cases} 1 & \text{if activity } \mathbf{A} \text{ is good regarding} \\ & \text{future generations' indicator } \mathbf{Fk;} \\ 0 & \text{if activity } \mathbf{A} \text{ is neutral regarding} \\ & \text{future generations' indicator } \mathbf{Fk;} \\ -2 & \text{if activity } \mathbf{A} \text{ is bad regarding} \\ & \text{future generations' indicator } \mathbf{Fk.} \end{cases}
$$

Fk(A) reflects the value of activity **A** to future generations regarding indicator **Fk**.

The following vector represents the value future generations award to activity **A** regarding the future generations' indicators **F1, . . . , Fk, . . . , Fn**.

(12) **F(A) = [F1(A), . . . , Fk(A), . . . , Fp(A)]**

To obtain an aggregate picture about the value future generations award to activity **A**, we must introduce *weights* that reflect the relative importance of indicators **F1, . . . , Fk, . . . , Fp**. Let **v1, . . . , vk, . . . , vp** be such importance weights.

It is required that:

(13) $\Sigma \; vk = 1$

The aggregate future generations' value of activity **A** can be calculated as follows:

(14) $F(A) = \Sigma \, vk \, Fk(A)$

F(A) thus reflects the aggregate value of activity **A** ($1 \geq$ **F(A)** ≥ -2) to future generations.

An activity can be considered *future respecting* if its aggregate value to future generations is positive. That is, if:

(15) $F(A) > 0$

The ancient moral law, "Love your neighbor as yourself" can be reinterpreted for organizations (business and non-business alike), as follows: "*Love Nature, Society and Future Generations as your own organizations.*" This commandment is realized if equations (5), (10) and (15) are simultaneously satisfied (Zsolnai 2003).

That is, if:

(16) $E(A), C(A), F(A) > 0$

The general responsibility of business and other organizations is to contribute to the conservation and restoration of the natural world, to the development of the capabilities of members of society and to respecting the freedom of future generations (Zsolnai 2006).

References

Ackoff, R. 2004: *Ackoff Center Guiding Principles*. Philadelphia: The Wharton School, University of Pennsylvania.

Azar, C. Holmberg, J. and Lindgren, K. 1996: "Socio-Ecological Indicators for Sustainability" *Ecological Economics* Vol. 18., pp. 89–112.

Brown Weiss, E. 1989: *In Fairness to Future Generations: International Law, Common Patrimony, and Intergeneration Equity*. The United Nations University, Tokyo & Transnational Publishers, Inc; Dobbs Ferry, New York.

Clark, M. J. 1916: "The Changing Basis of Economic Responsibility" *Journal of Political Economy* Vol. 24, No. 3., pp. 209–229.

Freeman, E., Harrison, J., Wicks, A., Parmar, B. and Colle, S. 2010: *Stakeholder Theory: The State of the Art*. Cambridge: Cambridge University Press.

Ims, K. J. and Zsolnai, L. 2009: "Holistic Problem Solving" in Zsolnai, L. and Tencati, A. (Eds.): *The Future International Manager: A Vision of the Roles and Duties of Management*. Basingstoke: Palgrave Macmillan. pp. 116–129.

Kahneman, D. 2011: *Thinking, Fast and Slow*. New York: Farrar, Straus and Giroux.

Leopold, A. 1948: *A Sand County Almanac*. Oxford: Oxford University Press.

Mitroff, I. 1998: *Smart Thinking for Crazy Times: The Art of Solving the Right Problems*. San Francisco: Berrett-Koehler Publishers, Inc.

Mitroff, I. and Silvers, A. 2009: *Dirty Rotten Strategies—How We Trick Ourselves and Others into Solving the Wrong Problems Precisely*. Palo Alto, CA: Stanford University Press.

Sen, A. 1992: *Inequality Re-examined*. Oxford: Clarendon Press.

Zsolnai, L. 2003: "Global Impact—Global Responsibility: Why a Global Management Ethos Is Necessary?" *Corporate Governance* No. 3, pp. 95–100.

Zsolnai, L. 2006: "Extended Stakeholder Theory" *Society and Business Review* Vol. 1, No. 1, pp. 37–44.

9 Economic Ethics and World Religions

Economics is mostly considered a worldly matter in which transcendence has no significance; consequently, there is no place for religion or spirituality in economics. However, from Max Weber's influential work "The Protestant Ethic and the Spirit of Capitalism" (Weber 1905) we know that religious beliefs and spirituality do play an important role in shaping economic systems and their development.

Jared L. Peifer (2015) suggests that we differentiate between four interinstitutional situations that can exist between religion and business, namely: engagement, co-optation, adjudication and disengagement. Engagement refers to when there is a strong moral religious authority over business, and the boundary between religion and business is blurred. In the case of co-optation, the boundary between religion and business is also blurred, but there is only weak (or non-existing) moral religious authority over business. Adjudication indicates that there is a strong moral religious authority over business, but religion and business are separate. Finally, in the case of disengagement, religion and business are separate and there is only weak (or non-existing) moral religious authority over business (Peifer 2015: 367).

The economic teachings of world religions challenge the way modern economies function, and often promote life-serving modes of economizing that support the livelihoods of human communities and the sustainability of natural ecosystems. As a result, they can inform and inspire spiritually grounded economic initiatives worldwide.

9.1 Jewish Economic Man

Meir Tamari has reconstructed the principles of Jewish economic ethics and the main features of the "Jewish Economic Man" (Tamari 1987, 1988).

Judaism considers the role of the entrepreneur as legitimate and desirable. Entrepreneurs are morally entitled to make profits in return for fulfilling their roles in society. The real problem is the challenge of *wealth*. How should

Jewish Economic Man use his or her wealth? What are his or her obligations to other members of the community, especially to the poor and disabled?

It is an axiom of Judaism that stronger and more successful members of a community have a duty to provide for those who do not share their prosperity. The Hebrew word for charity (*Tzedakah*) has the same root as the word for justice.

Jewish Economic Man should give 10–20% of his or her profit to *charity*—to help weaker and less successful members of the community.

The central teaching of Jewish Economic ethics is the insistence that one should *not cause damage*—directly, indirectly or even accidentally. As the rabbinic dictum says, "One has a benefit and other does not suffer a loss." This principle creates strict ecological and human constraints to economic activity. Jewish Economic Man must often choose second-best or third-best alternatives that do no harm.

In Judaism, man is the pinnacle of God's creation, so that everything exists for the benefit of humans. However, this imposes an obligation on men and women to hand over the world to *future generations* in a state that provides *equally well* for them.

In sum, we can say that Jewish Economic Man has two fundamental obligations. First, they can make a profit if and only if their enterprise does not harm anybody. Second, they should give a portion of profits they create to charity (see also Pava 2011).

9.2 Catholic Social Teaching

The Catholic vision of economic life is based on the *Social Teaching of the Church* (U.S. Bishops 1986, Mele 2011).

According to Christianity, *humans* are sacred because they are the clearest reflection of God on Earth. Human dignity comes from God, not from nationality, race, sex, economic status or any human accomplishments. Thus, every economic decision and institution must be judged according to whether it protects or undermines the *dignity* of human persons.

Catholic Social Teaching creates an interconnected web of duties, rights and priorities. First, *duties* are defined as love and justice. Corresponding to these duties are the *human rights* of every person. Finally, observance of duties and rights generates numerous *priorities* that should guide the economic choices of individuals, communities and the nation as a whole.

Love is at the heart of Christian morality: "Love thy neighbor as thyself." In the framework of contemporary decision theory, this commandment is formulated to mean that actors should give the same weight to others' payoffs as to their own.

Justice has three meanings in Catholic Social Teaching. Commutative justice calls for fairness in all agreements and exchanges between individuals and social groups. Distributive justice requires the allocation of income, wealth and power to persons whose basic needs are unmet. Finally, social justice implies the participation of every individual in economic and social life.

In Catholic Social Teaching, human rights play a fundamental role. Not only are well-known civil and political rights emphasized but also those concerning human welfare in general. Among these, 'economic rights' are the right to life, food, shelter, rest, medical care and basic education—because these rights are indispensable for the protection of human dignity.

The main priorities for the economy include the following:

(i)   Fulfillment of the basic needs of the poor;
(ii)   An increase in the participation of excluded and vulnerable people in economic life;
(iii)   Investment specifically to benefit the poor or economically insecure; and
(iv)   The creation of economic and social policies that protect the strength and stability of families.

Each individual is called on to contribute to the common good by seeking excellence in production and service. The freedom of business is protected, but the accountability of business to the common good and justice must be ensured. Government has an essential moral function: to protect human rights and secure justice for all members of society.

In sum, we can say that Catholic Social Teaching mandates that the economy should support the dignity of human persons. Economic activities are subordinated to this goal.

9.3 Islamic Economics

According to advocates of Islamic economics, economic life cannot be considered in isolation from society in general. Islamic economics is an integral part of Islamic governance. The principles of Islamic governance are derived from the *Sharia'h* (literally 'path'; i.e., the Divine Path or Law that all Muslims must follow) as revealed by Allah to his Messenger, the Prophet Muhammad, in the Qur'an, and the *Sunnah* (the actions and collected sayings, or *Hadith*) of the Prophet. Islam involves the submission of the individual to the Will of Allah (Khan 2011).

Kuran (2004) characterizes Islamic economics as having the following three basic tenets: (i) the prohibition of *riba* (i.e., interest or usury) in all financial transactions; (ii) wealth redistribution through the levy of *zakat* (a religious alms tax) on all movable wealth—this is usually levied at the rate of 2.5% per lunar year for most Muslims, although the exact rate varies; and (iii) adherence to Islamic economic norms that "command good" and "forbid evil"; this includes forbearing from products and activities deemed *haram* (forbidden) for Muslims, such as economic activities involving alcohol, pork, gambling or pornography.

Feisal Khan (2011) argues that Islamic economics is essentially transformative. Rather than being a process of simple normative economic analysis geared towards a desired economic outcome, Islamic economics, being a part of the Sharia'h, is structured to transform human beings to achieving higher goals (Zaman, 2008). The transformation of 'base' (i.e., self-centered) desires into the 'higher goals' of peace, improvement of human welfare and spirituality is key to Islamic economics.

In their pursuit of human transformation, Islamic economists have, among other goals, advocated for greater wealth and income equality; communal/public ownership of some key physical resources such as forests, mineral deposits and grazing lands; the immorality and illegality of business transactions where gains are disproportionately one-sided; and profit-sharing in good times and belt-tightening in bad times for all employees. Trading and making a profit is not only entirely legal, but highly encouraged, provided that it is done 'justly' (i.e., with commensurate risk-sharing, and without exploitation) (Khan 2011).

9.4 Hindu Economics

Hindu economic thinking can be traced back to Kautilya (350–275 BCE), but the concepts of Hindu economics were comprehensively expressed by M.K. Gandhi in the twentieth century. Gandhian economics rejects the goal of the maximization of material self-interest so central to modern economic thought. For Gandhi and his followers, the fulfillment of human needs should be at the center of economic functioning—including the need for meaning and community. Gandhian economics aims to promote spiritual development and harmony, and rejects materialism (Kumarappa 1951).

Gandhian economics has the following underlying values: (i) truth (*satya*), (ii) non-violence (*ahimsa*) and (iii) non-possession (*aparigraha*) (Ghosh 2007). Based on satya and ahimsa, Gandhi derived the principle of non-possession. Possession leads to violence (to protect one's possessions, and to acquire others' possessions), so Gandhi was clear that individuals should limit their needs to the basic minimum. He embodied this idea personally, as his worldly possessions only included his clothes, watch, stick and a few utensils. He advocated this principle to all, especially to the rich and the industrialists, arguing that they should see their wealth as something they held in trust for society.

The first basic principle of Gandhi's economic thought is that special emphasis should be placed on 'plain living,' which helps to cut down on wants, and on being *self-reliant*. The increasing appetites of consumers are thereby likened to the appetites of animals, which travel to the ends of the Earth in search of satisfaction. Thus a distinction should be made between 'Standard of Living' and 'Standard of Life,' wherein the former merely describes the material and physical standard of food, clothing and housing. A higher standard of life, on the other hand, can be attained only if, along with material advancement, there is a serious attempt to imbibe cultural and spiritual values and qualities (Diwan and Lutz (Eds.) 1987).

The second principle of Gandhian economic thought is the need to promote *small-scale* and *locally oriented production* that uses local resources and meets local needs, so that employment opportunities are created. This involves the use of technology that is labor-intensive rather than labor-saving. The Gandhian economy increases employment opportunities rather than decreases them. Gandhi was not in absolute opposition to the use of machinery; he welcomed it when it could be used to avoid drudgery and reduce tedium. He also emphasized the dignity of labor, and criticized society's contemptuous attitude to manual labor, insisting that everybody should do some 'bread labor' (Diwan and Lutz (Eds.) 1987).

The third principle of Gandhian economic thought is *trusteeship*. This means that individuals or groups of individuals should be free not only to make a decent living through economic enterprise, and also to accumulate wealth, but any surplus created beyond what is necessary to meet basic needs and make investments should be held in trust for the welfare of all, particularly the poorest and most deprived (Diwan and Lutz (Eds.) 1987).

Implementation of the three principles could minimize economic and social inequality, and achieve 'sarvodaya,' welfare for all, in contrast to welfare for a few.

9.5 Buddhist Economics

Buddhist economics is based on the Buddhist way of life. The main goal of Buddhist life is to reach a state of *liberation* from all suffering. *Nirvana* is the final state, which can be approached through negation of wants and the purification of human character.

Schumacher described Buddhist economics in his best-selling book *Small Is Beautiful* (Schumacher 1973).

The central values of Buddhist economics are *simplicity* and *non-violence*. From a Buddhist point of view, the optimal pattern of consumption involves creating a high level of satisfaction for humans through a low rate of material consumption. This will allow people to live without pressure and strain, and to fulfill the primary injunction of Buddhism: "Cease to do evil; try to do good." As natural resources are everywhere limited, people who live simple lifestyles are obviously less likely to be at each other's throats than those who are overly dependent on scarce natural resources.

According to Buddhist economics, production using local resources for local needs is the most rational way of organizing economic life. Dependence on imports from afar and the consequent need for export production is uneconomic, and justifiable only in exceptional cases.

For Buddhists there is an essential difference between renewable and non-renewable resources. Non-renewable resources must only be consumed if their use is absolutely indispensable, and then only with the greatest care and concern for conservation. To use non-renewable resources heedlessly or extravagantly is an act of violence. Economizing should be based on renewable resources as much as possible.

Buddhism does not accept the assumption of man's superiority over other species. Its motto can be described as 'noblesse oblige'; that is, man must be kind and compassionate towards natural creatures and be good to them in every way.

In sum, we can say that Buddhist economics represents a middle way between the modern, growth-focused economy and traditional stagnation. It is designed to foster the most appropriate path of development: 'Right Livelihoods' for people (see also Zsolnai (Ed.) 2011).

9.6 The Taoist Economy

Taoism and Confucianism greatly influence the economies of far-eastern countries. After studying Taiwan's economy, Li-teh Sun described the main features of the Taoist economy (Li-teh Sun 1986).

'Tao' is a fundamental concept that represents the path of equilibrium and harmony among the myriad things in the Universe. Taoists believe that two basic forces exist in the Universe: *yin* and *yang*. Yin is the feminine principle; the yielding, cooperative force. Yang is the masculine principle; the active, competitive force. Yin and yang are complementary. Humans need to find their own internal balance between yin and yang, as well as balance in society. This will result in the fulfillment of Tao.

In the Taoist economy, two basic concepts play decisive roles: the *inner equilibrium* of individuals and *social harmony*. The former is necessary for resolving microeconomic problems, while the latter is fundamental to handling macroeconomic issues.

At the microeconomic level, the following yin and yang pairs are balanced in the Taoist economy:

(i)   Public interest versus self-interest;
(ii) Morality versus profit;

(iii)   Want negation versus want satisfaction;
(iv)   Cooperation versus competition;
(v)   Leisure versus work.

In the Taoist economy, economic activity is not only fostered by self-interest, but also entrepreneurs should promote the supply of public goods and services, too. Profit should not be the sole incentive for work and investment. Because profit comes from society, some portion of it should be returned to society in the form of social responsibility. The Taoist consumer regulates their 'wants,' even when their income is not constrained. Want negation is valued, as the maximization of wants is unwise and has detrimental impacts on communities and the natural environment. In production, cooperative and competitive instincts are balanced. Competition without cooperation would create chaos, but cooperation without competition would generate poverty. Leisure and work are of equal importance to individuals. Work produces wealth, while leisure is necessary for moral development.

At the macroeconomic level, the following yin and yang pairs are balanced in the Taoist economy:

(i)   The poor versus the rich;
(ii)   Labor versus capital;
(iii) Public sector versus private sector;
(iv)   Planning system versus market system;
(v)   Stagnation versus growth;
(vi)   Full employment versus price stability.

Achieving balance between the poor and the rich requires the equitable distribution of income and wealth. Taoist social policy aims at the elimination of artificial inequalities among people, but does not try to eliminate natural inequalities altogether. The balance between labor and capital has two components: one is the right proportion of labor production and machine production, and the other is the right proportion of labor ownership and capital ownership. Balance between the public and the private sector is necessary because the public sector provides public goods and services, while the private sector promotes economic efficiency. Achieving a state of balance between the planning system and the market system is also important for similar reasons. Balance between stagnation and growth requires some reduction in the natural growth rate of the economy. In the Taoist economy, there is no trade-off between unemployment and inflation. Since yin and yang forces rule the economy, a balance between employment and price stability is feasible.

In sum, we can say that the Taoist economy is based on a balance of yin and yang forces and is designed to foster the inner equilibrium of individuals as well as social harmony (see also Allinson 2011).

9.7 A Comparative View

Table 9.1 summarizes the different responses of the world religions described earlier to the economic questions. Judaism, Catholicism, Islam, Hinduism, Buddhism, and Taoism-Confucianism represent *life-serving modes of economizing*, which promote the livelihoods of human communities and the sustainability of natural ecosystems.

The understanding of world religions from the perspective of economic ethics is based on a spiritual conception of man. Human beings are considered to be spiritual beings embodied in the physical world, with both materialistic and non-materialistic desires and motivations. Materialistic desires and outcomes are embedded in and evaluated against spiritual convictions and experiences.

Table 9.1 Conceptions of World Religions in Terms of Economic Ethics

	Basic Values	*Economic Means*
Judaism	Cause no harm, Solidarity	Constraints on profit making, Charity
Catholicism	Love, Justice	Personal excellence, Responsible enterprises, Duties of the government
Islam	Sharia'h, Submission of the individual to the Will of Allah	Prohibition of interest, Wealth redistribution through religious alms tax, Adherence to Islamic norms that command good and forbid evil
Hinduism	Truth Non-violence Non-possession	Self-reliance, Local production, Trusteeship
Buddhism	Simplicity, Non-violence	Reducing consumption, Using local resources
Taoism-Confucianism	Inner equilibrium Of the individual, Social harmony	Yin and yang forces At microeconomic and Macroeconomic levels

Many innovative economic practices have been inspired by the teachings of world religions, but the cases of Mondragon and Sarvoyada are especially interesting. The former is based on Catholic Social Teaching, and the latter on Gandhian economic principles.

9.8 The Mondragon Experience

Mondragon is a federation of worker cooperatives in the town of Mondragon in Basque Country, Spain, that was founded in 1956. It is the tenth-largest economic entity in Spain, and the leading business group in the Basque Country, with revenue of 11,479 million euros and total assets of 34,011 million euros in 2013. At the end of 2014, it employed 74,117 people in 257 companies and organizations in four main areas of activity: finance, industry, retail and knowledge management.

Mondragon was established by Catholic priest José María Arizmendiarrieta (1915–1976) in harmony with Catholic Social Teaching. Before creating the first cooperative, Arizmendiarrieta spent years educating young people about a form of humanism based on solidarity and participation, and the importance of acquiring the necessary technical knowledge. In 1955, he selected five of these young people to set up the cooperative's first company, which was the industrial beginning of the Mondragon Corporation.

Mondragon cooperatives are united by a humanist concept of business, a philosophy of participation and solidarity, and a shared business culture. Culture is rooted in a shared mission and a number of principles, corporate values and business policies. This framework of business culture has been structured based on a common culture derived from the basic 'Cooperative Principles' in which Mondragon is rooted. These include: Open Admission, Democratic Organization, the Sovereignty of Labor, the Instrumental and Subordinate Nature of Capital, Participatory Management, Payment Solidarity, Inter-cooperation, Social Transformation and Universality and Education.

This philosophy is complemented by four corporate values: Cooperation (acting as owners and protagonists), Participation (in the form of a commitment to management), Social Responsibility (distributing wealth based on solidarity) and Innovation (a focus on constant renewal in all areas of activity).

This business culture translates into compliance with a number of 'Basic Objectives' (Customer Focus, Development, Innovation, Profitability, People in Cooperation, and Involvement in the Community) and 'General Policies' that are approved by the 'Cooperative Congress' and are implemented and cascaded down to all of the corporation's organizational levels and incorporated into four-year strategic plans and the annual business plans of the individual cooperatives, divisions and the corporation as a whole.

At Mondragon, the wage ratio between executive work and field or factory work is pre-defined. These ratios range from 3:1 to 9:1 in different cooperatives, while the average is 5:1. That is, the general manager of an average Mondragon cooperative earns no more than five times as much as the minimum wage paid at their cooperative. The wage ratio of a cooperative is adjusted periodically by worker-owners through democratic voting.

In the field of finance, Mondragon activities include the banking businesses of Laboral Kutxa, the insurance company Seguros Lagun Aro and the voluntary social welfare body Lagun Aro. The yield derived from this fund is used to cover long-term retirement, widowhood and invalidity benefits, complementary to those offered by the Spanish social security system. Laboral Kutxa ended 2014 with revenue of 109.2 million euro after a year in which it granted loans worth 14.4 billion euro, mainly to households and small and medium-sized enterprises.

Mondragon companies manufacture consumer goods, capital goods, industrial components, products and systems for construction, and offer services to business. In the leisure and sports area, it manufactures Orbea bicycles, exercise equipment and items for camping, the garden and the beach. In 2014, cooperatives in the industrial sector created 1,000 jobs, and internationalization continued with 125 overseas production subsidiaries—three more than one year earlier.

Led by Eroski, Mondragon runs one of the leading retail groups in Spain, which operates throughout Spain and in southern France. At the end of 2013, Eroski was operating an extensive chain of 2,069 stores made up of 90 Eroski hypermarkets, 1,211 Eroski/centers, Caprabo, Eroski/city, Aliprox, Familia, Onda and Cash & Carry supermarkets, 155 branches of the Eroski/viajes travel agency, 63 petrol stations, 39 Forum Sport stores and 221 IF perfume stores. Moreover, in the south of France it has four hypermarkets, 16 supermarkets, 17 petrol stations, and four perfume stores in Andorra.

Mondragon's knowledge-production activity has a dual focus: training-education and innovation. Training-education is mainly linked to Mondragon University, which is a cooperative university that combines the development of knowledge, skills and values, and maintains close relations with business, especially Mondragon cooperatives. Technological innovation is generated through the cooperatives' own R&D departments, the 'Corporate Science and Technology Plan,' the corporation's 12 technology centers, and the Garaia Innovation Park.

Mondragon can be considered a successful alternative to the capitalist mode of production, and one in which efficiency is matched with solidarity and democracy. Vincent Navarro (2014) says,

> One of the successes of Mondragon was its ability to create a sense of identity among the workers within the company, encouraging an environment of solidarity and collegiality among them, a feeling that also extended (although to a much lesser degree) to non-worker-owners.

The Mondragon system provides evidence that cooperatives tend to last longer and are less susceptible to perverse incentives and other problems with organizational governance than more traditionally managed organizations (Sanchez Bajo and Roelants 2011).

9.9 The Sarvodaya Movement

Sarvodaya is Sri Lanka's largest people's organization. Over the last 50 years it has become a network of over 15,000 villages engaged in relief efforts and development projects.

Sarvodaya's total budget exceeds USD 5 million, with 1,500 full-time employees. When combined with numerous volunteer workers, the workforce comprises a full-time equivalent of approximately 200,000 individuals, placing Sarvodaya on a par with the entire plantation sector in Sri Lanka (Sarvodaya 2015).

Sarvodaya developed around a set of coherent philosophical tenets drawn from Buddhism and Gandhian thought. The visionary contributions of its founder and charismatic leader, Dr. A. T. Ariyaratne, continue to provide the organization with ideological and inspirational leadership, while day-to-day operations are in the hands of a new generation that is receptive to modern forms of management that are also compatible with the overall vision of this volunteer-based peoples' organization.

The Sarvodaya Shramadana Movement started in 1968. Sarvodaya is Sanskrit for 'awakening of all,' and Shramadana means 'to donate effort.' Initially, the movement took the form of an educational program designed to help students and teachers live and work with the most remote village communities in Sri Lanka where they developed self-help initiatives. Within nine years, however, the 'service-learning program' had expanded into a full-fledged development movement in hundreds of villages, with the goal of comprehensive and nonviolent social transformation. During its first 15 years, Sarvodaya expanded with hardly any foreign aid or state support, relying on volunteer labor, mostly from the beneficiaries themselves.

By the late 1970s, the Sarvodaya Movement, with support from partner organizations in more prosperous countries, became capable of reaching nearly every part of Sri Lanka. The program of self-reliance, community participation and a holistic approach to community 'awakening' appealed not only to people in poor communities but also to donors. Thousands of young women and men learned how to motivate and organize people in their own villages to meet basic human needs, ranging from a clean and adequate drinking-water supply to simple housing and sanitation, communications facilities, energy supply, education and methods of satisfying spiritual and cultural needs.

The momentum of the movement was such that by the early 1990s, in spite of harassment by the government and political violence, Sarvodaya was involved in enormous amounts of outreach activity. The movement's work now included peace building, conflict resolution and the development of technology and programs appropriate for children at risk, elders and those with disabilities—all the while maintaining its focus on taking a holistic approach to social mobilization through empowering individuals beyond mere economic development.

At approximately the same time, international priorities changed and the focus was placed on economic development strategy. Large projects and macro-interventions began to dominate the scene amongst donors, and Sarvodaya, which had originally attracted attention due to its broader philosophy, became a victim of its own success. In 1991, when 85% of external aid to the organization dried up, the movement was forced to go back to its roots. Since then, Sarvodaya has relied on so-called pioneer villages to provide support for the surrounding communities that still require development.

The Sarvodaya Shramadana Movement has now become stronger than ever. New administrative management at a national level is supporting a motivated group of emerging leaders at the village and district levels. Although almost one-third of the districts supported by Sarvodaya are not financed by outside partners, they are nevertheless surviving in the knowledge that, in the long-term, progress will come from partnerships and self-sustaining development activity rather than from charity. Sarvodaya's role in peacemaking, community building and increasing security in Sri Lanka is unique, and it continues to innovate in social, ethical, cultural, spiritual and economic fields.

Sarvodaya's efforts to promote development are not restricted to meeting basic needs such as clean drinking water, housing and access to basic education and health services. In the light of social 'awakening' and the need for the development of human potential, the movement also strives to increase the social and political participation of beneficiaries. This goal is visible in the comprehensive educational and training measures that the organization promotes to develop individual and community capacity for fostering self-determined and responsible development. Reaching a critical mass—one-third of all villages in Sri Lanka are involved in the Sarvodaya Movement—promotes social change, and therefore affects national development. The Sarvodaya model has in fact already influenced national policy strategies in certain areas, such as health and education (Sarvodaya 2015).

9.10   The Failures of the Materialistic Economic Man

Modern economics and business employ and promote a strongly materialistic conception of man. Human beings are considered to be body-mind encapsulated egos, with only materialistic desires and motivation. These kinds of creatures are modeled in traditional economics as 'Homo Oeconomicus,' which is the term used to describe an individualistic being who seeks to maximize his or her own self-interest. They are only interested in material utility as defined in monetary terms.

Modern economics and business presupposes the existence of monetary forms of extrinsic motivation, and suggests that success should only be measured in terms of profit. The economic and financial crisis of 2008–2009 has deepened our understanding of the problems of economic activities based on unlimited greed which cultivate an 'enrich yourself' mentality.

Based on the promotion of materialistic egoism, modern economies produce an enormous abundance of goods and services, but the ecological, social and psychological deficit they create is also huge.

Today, all advanced economies are significantly overshooting ecological boundaries. To live within the means of our planet's natural resources, a country's ecological footprint per person should not exceed the per person biocapacity. If a nation's ecological footprint per capita is higher than this figure, this indicates that its citizens are using more resources and creating more waste than our planet can regenerate and absorb. Data indicate that the most advanced countries use 200–500% of the environmental resources that their fair 'earth share' would permit.

Psychologists claim that a *materialistic value orientation* describes the priority that individuals give to goals such as money, possessions, image and status. Psychological research shows that the more people focus on materialistic goals, the less they tend to care about spiritual goals. Further, while most spiritual traditions seek to reduce personal suffering and encourage compassionate behavior, numerous studies document the fact that the more people prioritize materialistic goals, the *lower their personal well-being* and the more likely they are to engage in manipulative, competitive and ecologically degrading behaviors (Kasser 2011).

Luk Bouckaert writes that humans as 'Homo Spiritualis' should not be characterized in terms of their preferences and desire to maximize utility but by their awareness of being interconnected. This inter-existence of the self and the other cannot be reduced to concepts such as shared group interests or collective welfare functions. We are all interconnected on a level of being that is prior to our acting within and making the world. The spirit in each of us is the point of awareness when we feel connected to all other beings and to Being itself. This spiritual self-understanding is not a matter of abstract philosophical thinking, but a feeling of universal love and compassion that gives our lives and actions inner purpose and drive. It can transform the materialistic ego into a responsible and compassionate sense of self (Bouckaert 2011).

Materialistic economic and business models do not produce true wellbeing for people but actually undermine it. By advocating for action on the basis of money-making potential, and by justifying success in terms of profit, materialistic models of business encourage the irresponsible behavior of economic actors, contribute to ecological destruction and disregard the interests of future generations.

In acknowledging the primacy of the spiritual over the material, nonmaterialistic economic models may activate the intrinsic motivation of economic actors to serve the common good, and suggest that success should be measured in a multidimensional way. Such models promote the idea that profit and growth should not be considered final ends, but only elements of a broader set of goals. Similarly, cost-benefit calculations are not to be thought of as the only means of making economic decisions, but should be integrated into a more comprehensive scheme of wisdom-based economizing (Bouckaert and Zsolnai 2011).

References

Allinson, R. 2011: "Confucianism and Taoism" in Bouckaert, L. and Zsolnai, L. (Eds.): *The Palgrave Handbook of Spirituality and Business*. Basingstoke: Palgrave Macmillan. pp. 95–102.

Bouckaert, L. 2011: "Spirituality and Rationality" in Bouckaert, L. and Zsolnai, L. (Eds.): *The Palgrave Handbook of Spirituality and Business*. Basingstoke: Palgrave Macmillan. pp. 18–25.

Bouckaert, L. and Zsolnai, L. (Eds.) 2011: *The Palgrave Handbook of Spirituality and Business*. Basingstoke: Palgrave Macmillan.

Diwan, R. K. and Lutz, M. A. (Eds.) 1987: *Essays in Gandhian Economics*. Delhi: Gandhian Peace Foundation.

Ghosh, B. N. 2007: *Gandhian Political Economy: Principles, Practice and Policy*. Aldershot: Ashgate Publishing, Ltd.

Kasser, T. 2011: "Materialistic Value Orientation" in Bouckaert, L. and Zsolnai, L. (Eds.): *The Palgrave Handbook of Spirituality and Business*. Basingstoke: Palgrave Macmillan. pp. 204–211.

Khan, F. 2011: "Islamic Economics" in Bouckaert, L. and Zsolnai, L. (Eds.): *The Palgrave Handbook of Spirituality and Business*. Basingstoke: Palgrave Macmillan. pp. 138–146.

Kumarappa, J. C. 1951: *Gandhian Economic Thought*. Bombay: Library of Indian Economics.

Kuran, T. 2004: *Islam and Mammon: The Economic Predicaments of Islamism*. Princeton, NJ: Princeton University Press.

Mele, D. 2011: "Catholic Social Teaching" in Bouckaert, L. and Zsolnai, L. (Eds.): *The Palgrave Handbook of Spirituality and Business*. Basingstoke: Palgrave Macmillan. pp. 118–128.

Navarro, V. 2014: What About Cooperatives as a Solution? *The Case of Mondragon*, www.counterpunch.org/2014/04/30/the-case-of-mondragon/ (Accessed on October 25, 2015).

Pava, M. 2011: "Jewish Economic Perspective on Income and Wealth Distribution" in Bouckaert, L. and Zsolnai, L. (Eds.): *The Palgrave Handbook of Spirituality and Business*. Basingstoke: Palgrave Macmillan. pp. 111–117.

Peifer, J. L. 2015: "The Inter-Institutional Interface of Religion and Business" *Business Ethics Quarterly* Vol. 25, No. 3, pp. 363–391.

Sanchez Bajo, C. and Roelants, B. 2011: *Capital and the Debt Trap*. Basingstoke: Palgrave Macmillan.

Sarvodaya 2015: www.sarvodaya.org/ (Accessed on October 25, 2015).

Schumacher, E. F. 1973: *Small Is Beautiful*. London: Abacus.

Sun, Li-teh 1986: "Confucianism and the Economic Order of Taiwan" *International Journal of Social Economics* Vol. 13, No. 6, pp. 3–53.

Tamari, M. 1987: *With All Your Possessions: Jewish Ethics and Economic Life*. New York: The Free Press.

Tamari, M. 1988: *The Social Responsibility of the Corporation: A Jewish Perspective*. Bank of Israel.

U.S. Bishops 1986: Economic Justice for All. *Pastoral Letter on Catholic Social Teaching and the U.S. Economy*. Washington D.C.: United States Catholic Bishops.

Weber, M. 1905/2002: *The Protestant Ethic and the Spirit of Capitalism*. (Translated by Peter Baehr and Gordon C. Wells). London: Penguin Books.

Zaman, A. 2008: "Islamic Economics: A Survey of the Literature. Religion and Development Working Programme," Working Paper 22, International Development Department, University of Birmingham.

Zsolnai, L. (Ed.) 2011: *Ethical Principles and Economic Transformation—a Buddhist Approach*. New York: Springer.

10 Beyond Self

World-renowned organizational scholar James March of Stanford University once said that *undermining the doctrine of self-interest* may be the most important project of the twenty-first century (Zsolnai 2014). Self-interest is at the heart of economics, politics and everyday life. Individuals and organizations are encouraged to pursue their own self-interest without paying attention to the wider and longer-term consequences of their choices and actions. However, the extreme focus on the self by economic actors leads to the destruction of both material and non-material values.

Amartya Sen (1987) describes the structure of self-interested behavior by delineating its three distinct features: (i) self-centered welfare—when one's welfare depends only on one's own consumption; (ii) self-welfare goals—the goal is to maximize one's own welfare; and (iii) self-goal choice—one's choices are guided by the pursuit of one's goals.

These features are presently at the core of mainstream economic decision-making. A rich variety of evidence shows that self-interest-based activity and policies have detrimental impacts on nature, future generations and society at large. If we wish to survive and flourish in this material world we must transcend the self, and embrace wholeness. This value shift requires enormous changes in economics, politics and social life, but there seems to be no other option in view of the present state of ecological degradation and human suffering.

Peter Pruzan (2009) of the Copenhagen Business School states that post-materialistic, spiritually based leadership is emerging as an inclusive and holistic approach to business that integrates leaders' inner perspectives about identity, purpose, responsibility and success with their decisions and activities in the 'outer world' of business. Spiritual-based leadership can also be seen as an overarching term for other approaches, which are characterized by names such as 'business ethics,' 'values leadership,' 'corporate social responsibility' and 'sustainability,' although post-materialistic business considers ethics, social responsibility and sustainability not as instruments for protecting and promoting a classical business rationale, but as fundamental goals in their own right.

While traditional management aims to foster optimal economic performance subject to both self-imposed and societal constraints that mandate attention to the well-being of the organization's stakeholders, post-materialistic business essentially interchanges the means and ends. The 'why' of organizational existence is no longer economic growth, but the material and spiritual fulfillment of all those affected by an organization, although one major caveat to this is the requirement that the organization maintains and develops the economic capacity to serve its stakeholders.

Philosopher and economist Luk Bouckaert of the Catholic University of Leuven has formulated priorities for a post-materialistic economy as follows (Bouckaert 2011):

(i)   *Priority of basic needs over subjective preferences.* Preferences are individual and social constructions that express, intensify and transform basic needs, and in certain cases suppress and obstruct them. Basic needs, on the other hand, are the necessary preconditions for humane functioning in a historically and culturally determined community. One can translate basic needs into rights that one can claim on the basis of one's human dignity.

The classical objection to the 'basic needs' approach is that there is no consensus about the content of such needs. What people experience as basic needs, according to this perspective, depends precisely on individual preference. This critique is partially true. One cannot isolate basic needs from individual subjective aspirations, but this does not mean that basic needs should be reduced to those aspirations.

(ii) *Priority of commitment over self-interest.* Experimental economics and economic psychology empirically support the claim that social commitment takes moral priority over selfish behavior. Genuine commitment follows its own logic. One who selflessly devotes one's life to promoting justice desires something other than the pleasure of satisfying one's own altruistic preferences. He or she does it for the sake of justice itself, not (at least not primarily) as a means to an extrinsic end, such as increasing personal happiness or prestige. There is an essential difference between the instrumental function of a preference and the non-instrumental function of a commitment. While commitment seeks to bring about an identity or a way of being, preference satisfaction seeks advantage or pleasure.

(iii) *Priority of mutual trust over mutual advantage in the market.* A well-functioning market requires cooperation and mutual trust. The market instrumentalizes all values using the metric of individual, subjective preferences. When people determine values themselves, the lack of moral cohesion can open the way to far-reaching opportunistic behavior, which is in the long-term a threat to the satisfactory functioning of the market. Hence there is a growing awareness that moral self-regulation and 'social capital' in the form of mutual trust are constituents of a well-functioning market.

(iv) *Priority of economic democracy over shareholder capitalism.* Economic democracy is an alternative to bourgeois capitalism and to Marxist collectivism. Stakeholder management and co-creative entrepreneurship are highly valued in today's capitalist system. Business ethics criticizes shareholder capitalism and promotes the stakeholder theory of the firm. The strong version of stakeholder theory empowers stakeholders and makes them full partners in the firm, giving them the rights and claims of partners, thereby forming a community of co-responsible persons. In principle, an economic democracy is broader than a workers' democracy, while it aims at the balanced participation of all stakeholders.

References

Bouckaert, L. 2011: "Personalism" in Bouckaert, L. and Zsolnai, L. (Eds.): *The Palgrave Handbook of Spirituality and Business*. Basingstoke: Palgrave Macmillan. pp. 155–162.

Pruzan, P. 2009: *Rational, Ethical and Spiritual Perspectives on Leadership*. Oxford: Peter Lang.

Sen, A. 1987: *On Ethics and Economics*. Oxford: Blackwell.

Zsolnai, L. 2014: *Beyond Self: Ethical and Spiritual Dimensions of Economics*. Oxford: Peter Lang Academic Publishers.

Part V

The Richness of Life

11 Art Can Save the World

The core of market metaphysics is what Martin Heidegger (1978) calls 'calculative thinking.' In Heidegger's view, poetic thinking represented by genuine art is antagonistic towards this kind of thinking. Genuine art always represents 'poetic dwelling.'

To preserve nature and to satisfy real human needs, gentle, careful ways of undertaking economic activity are needed. Poetic dwelling models inspired by great art can influence organizations and people to transform themselves into *responsive* and *caring* agents.

11.1 The Poverty of Business Metaphysics

The metaphysics of modern-day business can be described by the following statements: (i) 'to be' is to be a marketable resource; (ii) 'to be' involves being either an object available for productive activity on the market or else a subject who makes use of such objects; and (iii) the only mode of thinking is calculative thinking—the consideration and measurement of every being as a marketable resource (Young 2002).

Such *market metaphysics*—what George Soros (1998) rightly calls 'market fundamentalism'—has a tendency to lead to the violation of nature and human beings. In many cases violent business practices result in 'essential' harm, such as the exploitation of forests for timber, the development of nuclear weapons designed to maim or exterminate life, or the commoditization of women as mere sex objects.

11.2 Genuine Art as an Alternative

The best modern art presents major challenges to modern business metaphysics. Joseph Beuys' famous performance, 'I like America, and America likes me,' is a prime example of the criticism of business civilization. In this compelling conceptual performance piece, Beuys flew to New York, was collected by ambulance and swathed in felt, then transported to a room in the Rene Block Gallery. This room was also occupied by a wild coyote, and for eight hours each day over a period of three days Beuys spent time with the coyote in the small room, with little more than the felt blanket wrapped around his entire body and a pile of straw. While in the room, the artist engaged in symbolist gestures, such as striking a triangle and tossing his gloves to the coyote. Beuys used copies of the *New York Times* to soak up the coyote's urine. At the end of the three days, the coyote, which had now become quite tolerant of Beuys, allowed the artist to hug it before he was transported back to the airport via ambulance. Despite his experience in the gallery with the coyote, Beuys did not set foot on American soil, nor did he see or explore the country (WikiArt 2014).

11.3 Gentle, Careful Ways of Economizing

Ecology and pro-socialness require gentle and caring economic actions. In such activities intrinsic motivation to serve the greater good is activated, and success is measured in multidimensional, holistic terms beyond the language of money.

Beauty reveals the shining of the spirit in the material world. The great paradox of values—as emphasized by British philosopher Roger Scruton (2011)—is that if utility considerations precede beauty and ethics, then utility itself will be destroyed. If we wish to live in a sustainable and human world, we should prioritize beauty and ethics over utility.

References

Bouckaert, L. and Zsolnai, L. (Eds.) 2011: *The Palgrave Handbook of Spirituality and Business*. Basingstoke: Palgrave Macmillan.

Heidegger, M. 1978: "The Question Concerning Technology" in Heidegger, M. (Ed.): *Basic Writings*. London: Routledge. pp. 307–342.

Scruton, R. 2011: *Beauty: A Very Short Introduction*. Oxford: Oxford University Press.

Soros, G. 1998. *The Crisis of Global Capitalism*. New York: Public Affairs.

WikiArt 2014: Joseph Beuys: *I Like America and America Likes Me*. www.wikiart. org/en/joseph-beuys/i-like-america-and-america-likes-me (Accessed on August 21, 2014).

Young, J. 2002: *Heidegger's Later Philosophy*. Cambridge: Cambridge University Press.

Index

Printed in the United States
by Baker & Taylor Publisher Services